HANDBOOK OF NATURE STUDY:

REPTILES, AMPHIBIANS, FISH AND INVERTEBRATES

COMPLETE YOUR COLLECTION TODAY!

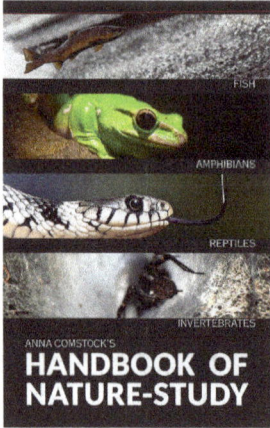

Reptiles, Amphibians,
Fish and Invertebrates

Birds

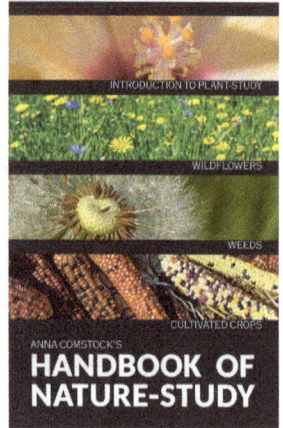

Wildflowers, Weeds
and Cultivated Crops

Mammals and
Flowerless Plants

Trees and
Garden Flowers

Earth and Sky

Insects

Introduction

Handbook of Nature-Study:

Reptiles, Amphibians, Fish and Invertebrates

ANNA BOTSFORD COMSTOCK, B.S., L.H.D

LATE PROFESSOR OF NATURE-STUDY IN CORNELL UNIVERSITY

LIVING BOOK
PRESS

This edition published 2020
by Living Book Press

ISBN: 978-1-922348-38-8 (hardcover)
         978-1-922348-39-5 (softcover)

A catalogue record for this book is available from the National Library of Australia

CONTENTS

THE TEACHING OF NATURE-STUDY

WHAT NATURE-STUDY IS

NATURE-STUDY is, despite all discussions and perversions, a study of nature; it consists of simple, truthful observations that may, like beads on a string, finally be threaded upon the understanding and thus held together as a logical and harmonious whole. Therefore, the object of the nature-study teacher should be to cultivate in the children powers of accurate observation and to build up within them, understanding.

WHAT NATURE-STUDY SHOULD DO FOR THE CHILD

FIRST, but not most important, nature-study gives the child practical and helpful knowledge. It makes him familiar with nature's ways and forces, so that he is not so helpless in the presence of natural misfortune and disasters.

Nature-study cultivates the child's imagination since there are so many wonderful and true stories that he may read with his own eyes, which affect his imagination as much as does fairy lore; at the same time nature-study cultivates in him a perception and a regard for what *is* true, and the power to express it. All things seem possible in nature; yet this seeming is always guarded by the eager quest of what is true. Perhaps, half the falsehood in the world is due to lack of power to detect the truth and to express it. Nature-study aids both in discernment and expression of things as they are.

Nature-study cultivates in the child a love of the beautiful; it brings to him early a perception of color, form and music. He sees whatever there is in his environment, whether it be the thunder-head piled up in the western sky, or the golden flash of the oriole in the elm; whether it be the purple of the shadows on the snow, or the azure glint on the wing of the little butterfly. Also, what there is of sound, he hears; he reads the music score of the bird orchestra, separating each part and knowing which bird sings it. And the patter of the rain, the gurgle of the brook, the sighing of the wind in the pine, he notes and loves and becomes enriched thereby.

But, more than all, nature-study gives the child a sense of companionship with life out of doors and an abiding love of nature. Let this latter be the teacher's criterion for judging his or her work. If nature-study as taught does not make the child love nature and the out-of-doors, then it should cease. Let us not inflict permanent injury on the child by turning him away from nature instead of toward it. However, if the love of nature is in the teacher's heart, there is no danger; such a teacher, no matter by what method, takes the child gently by the hand and walks with him in paths that lead to the seeing and comprehending of what he may find beneath his feet or above his head. And these paths whether they lead among the lowliest plants, or whether to

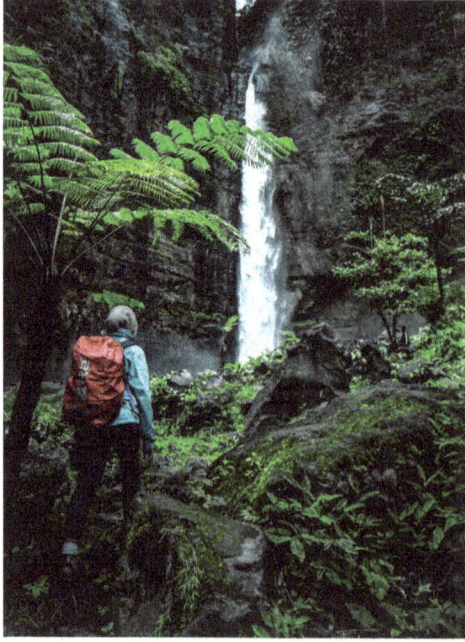

2

the stars, finally converge and bring the wanderer to that serene peace and hopeful faith that is the sure inheritance of all those who realize fully that they are working units of this wonderful universe.

NATURE-STUDY AS A HELP TO HEALTH

PERHAPS the most valuable practical lesson the child gets from nature-study is a personal knowledge that nature's laws are not to be evaded. Wherever he looks, he discovers that attempts at such evasion result in suffering and death. A knowledge thus naturally attained of the immutability of nature's "must" and "shall not" is in itself a moral education. That the fool as well as the transgressor fares ill in breaking natural laws, makes for wisdom in morals as well as in hygiene.

Out-of-door life takes the child afield and keeps him in the open air, which not only helps him physically and occupies his mind with sane subjects, but keeps him out of mischief. It is not only during childhood that this is true, for love of nature counts much for sanity in later life. This is an age of nerve tension, and the relaxation which comes from the comforting companionship found in woods and fields is, without doubt, the best remedy for this condition. Too many men who seek the out-of-doors for rest at the present time, can only find it with a gun in hand. To rest and heal their nerves they must go out and try to kill some unfortunate creature,—the old, old story of sacrificial blood. Far better will it be when, through properly training the child, the man shall be enabled to enjoy nature through seeing how creatures live rather than watching them die. It is the sacred privilege of nature-study to do this for future generations and for him thus trained, shall the words of Longfellow's poem to Agassiz apply:

"And he wandered away and away, with Nature the dear old nurse,
Who sang to him night and day, the rhymes of the universe.
And when the way seemed long, and his heart began to fail,
She sang a more wonderful song, or told a more wonderful tale."

WHAT NATURE-STUDY SHOULD DO FOR THE TEACHER

DURING many years, I have been watching teachers in our public schools in their conscientious and ceaseless work; and so far as I can foretell, the fate that awaits them finally is either nerve exhaustion or nerve atrophy. The teacher must become either a neurasthenic or a "clam."

I have had conversations with hundreds of teachers in the public schools of New York State concerning the introduction of nature-study into the curriculum, and most of them declared, "Oh, we have not time for it. Every moment is full now!" Their nerves were at such a tension that with one more thing to do they must fall apart. The question in my own mind during these conversations was always, how long can she stand it! I asked some of them, "Did you ever try a vigorous walk in the open air in the open country every Saturday or every Sunday of your teaching year?" "Oh no!" they exclaimed in despair of making me understand. "On Sunday we must go to church or see our friends and on Saturday we must do our shopping or our sewing. We must go to the dressmaker's lest we go unclad, we must mend, and darn stockings; we need Saturday to catch up."

Yes, catch up with more cares, more worries, more fatigue, but not with more growth, more strength, more vigor and more courage for work. In my belief, there are two and only two occupations for Saturday afternoon or forenoon for a teacher. One is to be out of doors and the other is to lie in bed, and the first is best. Out in this, God's beautiful world, there is everything waiting to heal lacerated nerves, to strengthen tired muscles, to please and content the soul that is torn to shreds with duty and care. To the teacher who turns to nature's healing, nature-study in the schoolroom is not a trouble; it is a sweet, fresh breath of air blown across the heat of radiators and the noisome odor of over-crowded small humanity. She, who opens her eyes and her heart nature-ward even once a week, finds nature-study in the schoolroom a delight and an abiding joy. What does such a one find in her schoolroom instead of the terrors of discipline, the eternal watching and eternal nagging to keep the pupils quiet and at work? She finds, first of all, companionship with her children; and second, she finds that without planning or going on a far voyage, she has found health and strength.

WHEN AND WHY THE TEACHER SHOULD SAY "I DO NOT KNOW"

NO SCIENCE professor in any university, if he be a man of high attainment, hesitates to say to his pupils, "I do not know," if they ask for information beyond his knowledge. The greater his scientific reputation and erudition, the more readily, simply and without apology he says this. He, better than others, comprehends how vast is the region that lies beyond man's present knowledge. It is only the teacher in the elementary schools who has never received enough scientific training to reveal to her how little she does know, who feels that she must appear to know everything or her pupils will lose confidence in her. But how useless is this pretence, in nature-study! The pupils, whose younger eyes are much keener for details than hers, will soon discover her limitations and then their distrust of her will be real.

In nature-study any teacher can with honor say, "I do not know;" for perhaps, the question asked is as yet unanswered by the great scientists. But she should not let her lack of knowledge be a wet blanket thrown over her pupils' interest. She should say frankly, "I do not know; let us see if we cannot together find out this mysterious thing. Maybe no one knows it as yet, and I wonder if you will discover it before I do." She thus conveys the right impression, that only a little about the intricate life of plants and animals is yet known; and at the same time she makes her pupils feel the thrill and zest of investigation. Nor will she lose their respect by doing this, if she does it in the right spirit. For three years, I had for comrades in my walks afield, two little children and they kept me busy saying, "I do not know." But they never lost confidence in me or in my knowledge; they simply gained respect for the vastness of the unknown.

The chief charm of nature-study would be taken away if it did not lead us through the border-land of knowledge into the realm of the undiscovered. Moreover, the teacher, in confessing her ignorance and at the same time her interest in a subject, establishes between herself and her pupils a sense of

SHISHIRDASIKA (CC BY-SA 4.0)
Spurred Butterfly Pea

companionship which relieves the strain of discipline, and gives her a new and intimate relation with her pupils which will surely prove a potent element in her success. The best teacher is always one who is the good comrade of her pupils.

NATURE-STUDY, THE ELIXIR OF YOUTH

THE old teacher is too likely to become didactic, dogmatic and "bossy" if she does not constantly strive with herself. Why? She has to be thus five days in the week and, therefore, she is likely to be so seven. She knows arithmetic, grammar and geography to their uttermost and she is never allowed to forget that she knows them, and finally her interests become limited to what she knows.

After all, what is the chief sign of growing old? Is it not the feeling that we know all there is to be known? It is not years which make people old; it is ruts, and a limitation of interests. When we no longer care about anything except our own interests, we are then old, it matters not whether our years be twenty or eighty. It is rejuvenation for the teacher, thus growing old, to stand ignorant as a child in the presence of one of the simplest of nature's miracles—the formation of a crystal, the evolution of the butterfly from the caterpillar, the exquisite adjustment of the silken lines in the spider's orb-web. I know how to "make magic" for the teacher who is growing old. Let her go out with her youngest pupil and fall on her knees before the miracle of the blossoming violet and say: "Dear Nature, I know naught of the wondrous life of these, your smallest creatures. Teach me!" and she will suddenly find herself young.

NATURE STUDY AS A HELP IN SCHOOL DISCIPLINE

MUCH of the naughtiness in school is a result of the child's lack of interest in his work, augmented by the physical inaction that results from an attempt to sit quietly. The best teachers try to obviate both of these rather than to punish because of them. Nature-study is an aid in both respects, since it keeps the child interested and also gives him something to do.

In the nearest approach to an ideal school that I have ever seen, for children of second grade, the pupils were allowed, as a reward of merit, to visit the aquaria or the terrarium for periods of five minutes, which time was given to the blissful observation of the fascinating prisoners. The teacher also allowed the reading of stories about the plants and animals under observation to be regarded as a reward of merit. As I entered the schoolroom, there were eight or ten of the children at the windows watching eagerly what was happening to the creatures confined there in the various cages. There was a mud aquarium for the frogs and salamanders, an aquarium for fish, many small aquaria for insects and each had one or two absorbingly interested spectators who were quiet, well behaved and were getting their nature-study lessons in an ideal manner. The teacher told me that the problem of discipline was solved by this method, and that she was rarely obliged to rebuke or punish. In many other schools, watching the living creatures in the aquaria, or terrarium has been used as a reward for other work well done.

THE RELATION OF NATURE-STUDY TO SCIENCE

NATURE-STUDY is not elementary science as so taught, because its point of attack is not the same; error in this respect has caused many a teacher to abandon nature-study and many a pupil to hate it. In elementary science the work begins with the simplest animals and plants and progresses logically through to the highest forms; at least this is the method pursued in most universities and schools. The object of the study is to give the pupils an outlook over all the forms of life and their relation one to another. In nature-study the work begins with any plant or creature which chances to interest the pupil. It begins with the robin when it comes back to us in March, promising spring; or it begins with the maple leaf which flutters to the ground in all the beauty of its autumnal tints. A course in biological science leads to the comprehension of all kinds of life upon our globe. Nature-study is for the comprehension of the individual life of the bird, insect or plant that is nearest at hand.

Nature-study is perfectly good science within its limits, but it is not meant to be more profound or comprehensive than the capabilities of the child's mind. More than all, nature-study is not science belittled as if it were to be looked at through the reversed opera glass in or-

An Aquarium

der to bring it down small enough for the child to play with. Nature-study, as far as it goes, is just as large as is science for "grown-ups" and may deal with the same subject matter and should be characterized by the same accuracy. It simply does not go so far.

To illustrate: If we are teaching the science of ornithology, we take first the Archaeopteryx, then the swimming and the scratching birds and finally reach the song birds, studying each as a part of the whole. Nature-study begins with the robin because the child sees it and is interested in it and he notes the things about the habits and appearance of the robin that may be perceived by intimate observation. In fact, he discovers for himself all that the most advanced book of ornithology would give concerning the ordinary habits of this one bird; the next bird studied may be the turkey in the barnyard, or the duck on the pond, or the screech-owl in the spruces, if any of these happen to impinge upon his notice and interest. However, such nature-study makes for the best of scientific ornithology, because by studying the individual birds thus thoroughly, the pupil finally studies a sufficient number of forms so that his knowledge, thus assembled, gives him a better comprehension of birds as a whole than could be obtained by the routine study of the same. Nature-study does not start out with the classification given in books, but in the end it builds up a classification in the child's mind which is based on fundamental knowledge; it is a classification like that evolved by the first naturalists, it is built on careful personal observations of both form and life.

NATURE-STUDY NOT FOR DRILL

IF nature-study is made a drill, its pedagogic value is lost. When it is properly taught, the child is unconscious of mental effort or that he is suffering the act of teaching. As soon as nature-study becomes a task, it should be dropped; but how could it ever be a task to see that the sky is blue, or the dandelion golden, or to listen to the oriole in the elm!

THE CHILD NOT INTERESTED IN
NATURE-STUDY

WHAT to do with the pupil not interested in nature-study subjects is a problem that confronts many earnest teachers. Usually the reason for this lack of interest, is the limited range of subjects used for nature-study lessons. Often the teacher insists upon flowers as the lesson subject, when toads or snakes would prove the key to the door of the child's interest. But whatever the cause may be, there is only one right way out of this difficulty: The child not inter-

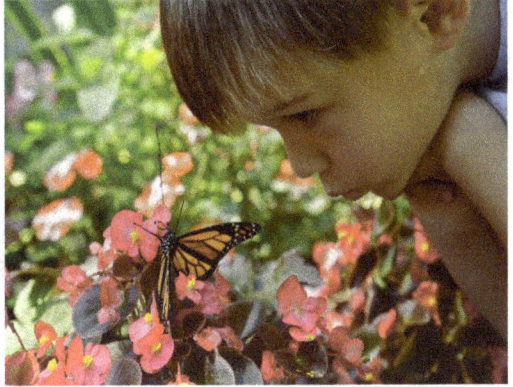
A young entomologist

ested should be kept at his regular school work and not admitted as a member of the nature-study class, where his influence is always demoralizing. He had much better be learning his spelling lesson than learning to hate nature through being obliged to study subjects in which he is not interested. In general, it is safe to assume that the pupil's lack of interest in nature-study is owing to a fault in the teacher's method. She may be trying to fill the child's mind with facts when she should be leading him to observe these for himself, which is a most entertaining occupation for the child. It should always be borne in mind that mere curiosity is always impertinent, and that it is never more so than when exercised in the realm of nature. A genuine interest should be the basis of the study of the lives of plants and lower animals. Curiosity may elicit facts, but only real interest may mold these facts into wisdom.

WHEN TO GIVE THE LESSON

THERE are two theories concerning the time when a nature-study lesson should be given. Some teachers believe that it should be a part of the regular routine; others have found it of greatest value if reserved for that period of the school day when the pupils are weary and restless, and the teacher's nerves strained to the snapping point. The lesson on a tree, insect or flower at such a moment affords immediate relief to everyone; it is a mental excursion, from which all return refreshed and ready to finish the duties of the day.

While I am convinced that the use of the nature-study lesson for mental refreshment makes it of greatest value, yet I realize fully that if it is relegated to such periods, it may not be given at all. It might be better to give it a regular period late in the day, for there is strength and sureness in regularity. The teacher is much more likely to prepare herself for the lesson, if she knows that it is required at a certain time.

THE LENGTH OF THE LESSON

THE nature-study lesson should be short and sharp and may vary from ten minutes to a half hour in length. There should be no dawdling; if it is an observation lesson, only a few points should be noted and the meaning for the observations made clear. If an outline be suggested for field observation, it should be given in an inspiring manner which shall make each pupil anxious to see and read the truth for himself. The nature story when properly read is never finished; it is always at an interesting point, "continued in our next."

The teacher may judge as to her own progress in nature-study by the length of time she is glad to spend in reading from nature's book what is therein written. As she progresses, she finds those hours spent in studying nature speed faster, until a day thus spent seems but an hour. The author can think of nothing she would so gladly do as to spend days and months with the birds, bees and flowers with no obligation for telling what she should see. There is more than mere information in hours thus spent. Lowell describes them well when he says:

"Those old days when the balancing of a yellow butterfly o'er a thistle bloom
Was spiritual food and lodging for the whole afternoon."

THE NATURE-STUDY LESSON ALWAYS NEW

A nature-study lesson should not be repeated unless the pupils demand it. It should be done so well the first time that there is no need of repetition, because it has thus become a part of the child's consciousness. The repetition of the same lesson in different grades was, to begin with, a hopeless incubus upon nature-study. One disgusted boy declared, "Darn germination! I had it in the primary and last year and now I am having it again. I know *all about germination.*" The boy's attitude was a just one; but if there had been revealed to him the meaning of germination, instead of the mere process, he would have realized that until he had planted and observed every plant in the world he would not know all about germination, because each seedling has its own interesting story. The only excuse for repeating a nature-study lesson is in recalling it for comparison and contrast with other lessons. The study of the violet will naturally bring about a review of the pansy; the dandelion, of the sunflower; the horse, of the donkey; the butterfly, of the moth.

NATURE-STUDY AND OBJECT LESSONS

THE object lesson method was introduced to drill the child to see a thing accurately, not only as a whole, but in detail and to describe accurately what he saw. A book or a vase or some other object was held up before the class for a moment and then removed; afterwards the pupils described it as perfectly as possible. This is an excellent exercise and the children usually enjoy it as if it were a game. But if the teacher has in mind the same thought when she is giving the nature-study lesson, she has little comprehension of the meaning of the latter

A mountain stream

and the pupils will have less. In nature-study, it is not desirable that the child see all the details, but rather those details that have something to do with the life of the creature studied; if he sees that the grasshopper has the hind legs much longer than the others, he will inevitably note that there are two other pairs of legs and he will in the meantime have come into an illuminating comprehension of the reason the insect is called "grasshopper." The child should see definitely and accurately all that is necessary for the recognition of a plant or animal; but in nature-study, the observation of form is for the purpose of better understanding life. In fact, it is form linked with life, the relation of "being" to "doing."

NATURE-STUDY IN THE SCHOOLROOM

MANY subjects for nature-study lessons may be brought into the schoolroom. Whenever it is possible, the pupils should themselves bring the material, as the collecting of it is an important part of the lesson. There should be in the schoolroom conveniences for caring for the little prisoners brought in from the field. The terrarium and breeding cages of different kinds should be provided for the insects, toads and little mammals. Here they may live in comfort, when given their natural food, while the children observe their interesting ways. The ants' nest, and the observation hive yield fascinating views of the marvelous lives of the insect socialists, while the cheerful prisoner in the bird cage may be made a constant illustration of the adaptations and habits of all birds. The aquaria for fishes, tadpoles and insects afford the opportunity for continuous study of these water creatures and are a never-failing source of interest to the pupils, while the window garden may be made not only an ornament and an aesthetic

Observing bees

delight, but a basis for interesting study of plant growth and development.

A schoolroom thus equipped is a place of delight as well as enlightenment to the children. Once, a boy whose luxurious home was filled with all that money could buy and educated tastes select, said of a little nature-study laboratory which was in the unfinished attic of a school building, but which was teeming with life: "I think this is the most beautiful room in the world."

NATURE-STUDY AND MUSEUM SPECIMENS

THE matter of museum specimens is another question for the nature-study teacher to solve, and has a direct bearing on an attitude toward taking life. There are many who believe the stuffed bird or the case of pinned insects have no place in nature-study; and certainly these should not be the chief material. But let us use our common sense; the boy sees a bird in the woods or field and does not know its name; he seeks the bird in the museum and thus is able to place it and read about it and is stimulated to make other observations concerning it. Wherever the museum is a help to the study of life in the field, it is well and good. Some teachers may give a live lesson from a stuffed specimen, and other teachers may stuff their pupils with facts about a live specimen; of the two, the former is preferable.

There is no question that making a collection of insects is an efficient way of developing the child's powers of close observation, as well as of giving him manual dexterity in handling fragile things. Also it is a false sentiment which attributes to an insect the same agony at being impaled on a pin that we might suffer at being thrust through by a stake. The

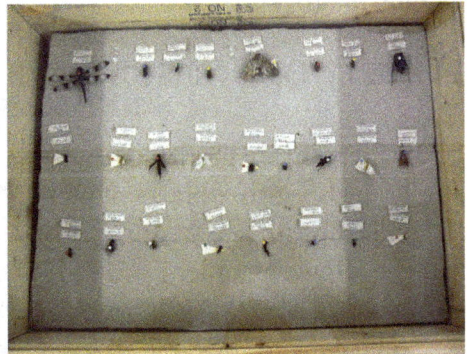

BENNY MAZUR (CC BY-SA 2.0)
Mounted insects in a box

insect nervous system is far more conveniently arranged for such an ordeal than ours; and, too, the cyanide bottle brings immediate and

13

painless death to the insects placed within it; moreover, the insects usually collected have short lives anyway. So far as the child is concerned, he is thinking of his collection of moths or butterflies and not at all of taking life; so it is not teaching him to wantonly destroy living creatures. However, an indiscriminate encouragement of the making of insect collections cannot be advised. There are some children who will profit by it and some who will not, and unquestionably the best kind of study of insects is watching their interesting ways while they live.

To kill a creature in order to prepare it for a nature-study lesson is not only wrong but absurd, for nature-study has to do with life rather than death, and the form of any creature is interesting only when its adaptations for life are studied. But again, a nature-study teacher may be an opportunist; if without any volition on her part or the pupils', a freshly killed specimen comes to hand, she should make the most of it. The writer remembers most illuminating lessons from a partridge that broke a window and its neck simultaneously during its flight one winter night, a yellow hammer that killed itself against an electric wire, and a muskrat that turned its toes to the skies for no understandable reason. In each of these cases the creature's special physical adaptations for living its own peculiar life were studied, and the effect was not the study of a dead thing, but of a successful and wonderful life.

THE LENS, MICROSCOPE, AND FIELD GLASS AS HELPS IN NATURE-STUDY

IN elementary grades, nature-study deals with objects which the children can see with the naked eye. However, a lens is a help in almost all of this work because it is such a joy to the child to gaze at the wonders it reveals. There is no lesson given in this book which requires more than a simple lens for seeing the most minute parts

Using a hand lens

discussed. An excellent lens may be bought for a dollar, and a fairly good one for fifty cents or even twenty-five cents. The lens should be chained to a table or desk where it may be used by the pupils at recess. This gives each an opportunity for using it and obviates the danger of losing it. If the pupils

Binoculars

themselves own lenses, they should be fastened by a string or chain to the pocket.

A microscope has no legitimate part in nature-study. But if there is one available, it reveals so many wonders in the commonest objects, that it can be made a source of added interest ofttimes. For instance, to thus see the scales on the butterfly's wing affords the child pleasure as well as edification. Field or opera glasses, while indispensible for bird study, are by no means necessary in nature-study. However, the pupils will show greater interest in noting the birds' colors if they are allowed to make the observations with the help of a glass.

USES OF PICTURES, CHARTS, AND BLACKBOARD DRAWINGS

PICTURES alone should never be used as the subjects for nature-study lessons, but they may be of great use in illustrating and illuminating a lesson. Books well illustrated are more readily comprehended by the child and are often very helpful to him, especially after his interest in the subject is thoroughly aroused. If charts are used to illustrate the lesson, the child is likely to be misled by the size of the drawing, which is also the case in blackboard pictures. However, this error may be avoided by fixing the attention of the pupil on the object first. If the pupils are studying the ladybird and have it in their hands, the teacher may use a diagram representing the beetle as a foot long and it will still convey the idea accurately; but if she begins with the picture, she probably can never convince the children that the picture has anything to do with the insect.

In making blackboard drawings illustrative of the lesson, it is best, if possible, to have one of the pupils do the drawing in the presence of the class; or, if the teacher does the drawing, she should hold the object in her hand while doing it and look at it often so that the children may see that she is trying to represent it accurately. Taking everything into consideration, however, nature-study charts and blackboard drawings are of little use to the nature-study teacher.

THE USES OF SCIENTIFIC NAMES

DISQUIETING problems relative to scientific nomenclature always confront the teacher of nature-study. My own practice has been to use the popular names of species, except in cases where confusion might ensue, and to use the scientific names for anatomical parts. However, this matter is of little importance if the teacher bears in mind that the purpose of nature-study is to know the subject under observation and to learn the name incidentally.

If the teacher says: "I have a pink hepatica. Can anyone find me a blue one?" the children, who naturally like grown-up words, will soon be calling these flowers hepaticas. But if the teacher says, "These flowers are called hepaticas. Now please everyone remember the name. Write it in your books as I write it on the blackboard,

Common tree frog or tree toad, Hyla versicolor. *Another species,* Hyla crucifer, *is also often called the tree frog and tree toad. Common names, then, will not distinguish these amphibians one from another; the scientific names must be applied.*

and in half an hour I shall ask you again what it is," the pupils naturally look upon the exercise as a word lesson and its real significance is lost. This sort of nature-study is dust and ashes and there has been too much of it. The child should never be *required* to learn the name of anything in the nature-study work; but the name should be used so often and so naturally in his presence, that he will learn it without being conscious of the process.

THE STORY AS A SUPPLEMENT TO THE
NATURE-STUDY LESSON

MANY of the subjects for nature lessons can be studied only in part, since but one phase may be available at the time. Often, especially if there is little probability that the pupils will find opportunity to complete the study, it is best to round out their knowledge by reading or telling the story to supplement the facts which they have discovered for themselves. This story should not be told as a finality or as a complete picture but as a guide and inspiration for further study. Always leave at the end of the story an interrogation mark that will remain aggressive and insistent in the child's mind. To illustrate: Once a club of junior naturalists brought me rose leaves injured by the leaf-cutter bee and asked me why the leaves were cut out so regularly. I told them the story of the use made by the mother bee of these oval and circular bits of leaves and made the account as vital as I was able; but at the end I said, "I do not know which species of bee cut these leaves. She is living here among us and building her nest with your rose leaves which she is cutting every day almost under your very eyes. Is she then so much more clever than you that you cannot see her nor find her nest?" For two years following this lesson I received letters from members of this club. Two carpenter bees and their nests were discovered by them and studied before the mysterious leaf-cutter was finally ferreted out. My story had left something interesting for the young naturalists to discover. The children should be impressed with the fact that the nature story is never finished. There is not a weed nor an insect nor a tree so common that the child, by observing carefully, may not see things never yet recorded in scientific books; therefore the supplementary story should be made an inspiration for keener interest and

GAIL HAMPSHIRE (CC BY-SA 2.0)
The leaf-cutter bee

further investigation on the part of the pupil. The supplementary story simply thrusts aside some of the obscuring underbrush thus revealing more plainly the path to further knowledge.

THE NATURE-STUDY ATTITUDE TOWARD LIFE AND DEATH

PERHAPS no greater danger besets the pathway of the nature-study teacher than the question involved in her pupils' attitude toward life and death. To inculcate in the child a reverence for life and yet to keep him from becoming mawkish and morbid is truly a problem. It is almost inevitable that the child should become sympathetic with the life of the animal or plant studied, since a true understanding of the life of any creature creates an interest which stimulates a desire to protect this particular creature and make its life less hard. Many times, within my own experience, have I known boys, who began by robbing birds' nests for egg collections, to end by becoming most zealous protectors of the birds. The humane qualities within these boys budded and blossomed in the growing knowledge of the lives of the birds. At Cornell University, it is a well known fact that those students who turn aside so as not to crush the ant, caterpillar or cricket on the pavement are almost invariably those that are studying entomology; and in America it is the botanists themselves who are leading the crusade for flower protection.

Thus, the nature-study teacher, if she does her work well, is a sure aid in inculcating a respect for the rights of all living beings to their own lives; and she needs only to lend her influence gently in this direction to change carelessness to thoughtfulness and cruelty to kindness. But with this impetus toward a reverence for life, the teacher soon finds herself in a dilemma from which there is no logical way out, so long as she lives in a world where lamb chop, beefsteak and roast chicken are articles of ordinary diet; a world in fact, where every meal is based upon the death of some creature. For if she places much emphasis upon the sacredness of life, the children soon begin to question whether it be right to slay the lamb or the chicken for their own food. It would seem that there is nothing for the consistent nature-study teacher to do but become a vegetarian, and even then there might arise refinements in this question of taking life; she might have to consider the cruelty to asparagus in cutting it off in plump infancy, or the ethics of devouring in the turnip the food laid up by the mother plant to perfect her seed. In fact, a most rigorous diet would be forced upon the teacher who should refuse to sustain her own existence at

18

the cost of life; and if she should attempt to teach the righteousness of such a diet she would undoubtedly forfeit her position; and yet what is she to do! She will soon find herself in the position of a certain lady who placed sheets of sticky fly-paper around her kitchen to rid her house of flies, and then in mental anguish picked off the buzzing, struggling victims and sought to clean their too adhesive wings and legs.

In fact, drawing the line between what to kill and what to let live, requires the use of common sense rather than logic. First of all, the nature-study teacher, while exemplifying and encouraging the humane attitude toward the lower creatures, and repressing cruelty which wantonly causes suffering, should never magnify the terrors of death. Death is as natural as life and the inevitable end of physical life on our globe. Therefore, every story and every sentiment expressed which makes the child feel that death is terrible, is wholly wrong. The one right way to teach about death is not to emphasize it one way or another, but to deal with it as a circumstance common to all; it should be no more emphasized than the fact that creatures eat or fall asleep.

Another thing for the nature-study teacher to do is to direct the interest of the child so that it shall center upon the hungry creature rather than upon the one which is made into the meal. It is well to emphasize the fact that one of the conditions imposed upon every living being in the woods and fields, is that it is entitled to a meal when it is hungry, if it is clever enough to get it. The child naturally takes this view of it. I remember well as a child I never thought particularly about the mouse which my cat was eating; in fact, the process of transmuting mouse into cat seemed altogether proper, but when the cat played with the mouse, that was quite another thing, and was never permitted. Although no one appreciates more deeply than I the debt which we owe to Thompson-Seton and writers of his kind, who have placed before the public the animal story from the animal point of view and thus set us all to thinking, yet it is certainly wrong to impress this view too strongly upon the young and sensitive child. In fact, this process should not begin until the judgment and the understanding is well developed, for we all know that although seeing the other fellow's standpoint is a source of strength and breadth of mind, yet living the other fellow's life is, at best, an enfeebling process and a futile waste of energy.

SHOULD THE NATURE-STUDY TEACHER TEACH
HOW TO DESTROY LIFE?

IT IS probably within the proper scope of the nature-study teacher to place emphasis upon the domain of man, who being the most powerful of all animals, asserts his will as to which ones shall live in his midst. From a standpoint of abstract justice, the stray cat has just as much right to kill and eat the robin which builds in the vine of my porch as the robin has to pull and eat the earthworms from my lawn; but the place is mine, and I choose to kill the cat and preserve the robin.

When emphasizing the domain of man, we may have to deal with the killing of creatures which are injurious to his interests. Nature-study may be tributary to this, in a measure, and indirectly, but it is surely *not* nature-study. For example, the child studies the cabbage butterfly in all its stages, the exquisitely sculptured yellow egg, the velvety green caterpillar, the chrysalis with its protecting colors, the white-winged butterfly, and becomes interested in the life of the insect. Not under any consideration, when the attention of the child is focused on the insect, should we suggest a remedy for it when a pest. Let the life-story of the butterfly stand as a fascinating page of nature's book. But later, when the child enters on his career as a gardener, when he sets out his row of cabbage plants and waters and cultivates them, and does his best to bring them to maturity, along comes the butterfly, now an arch enemy, and begins to rear her progeny on the product of his toil. Now the child's interest is focused on the cabbage, and the question is not one of killing insects so much as of saving plants. In fact, there is nothing in spraying the plants with Paris green which suggests cruelty to innocent caterpillars, nor is the process likely to harden the child's sensibilities.

To gain knowledge of the life-story of insects or other creatures is nature-study. To destroy them as pests is a part of Agriculture or Horticulture. The one may be of fundamental assistance to the other, but the two are quite separate and should never be confused.

THE FIELD NOTEBOOK

A field note-book may be made a joy to the pupil and a help to the teacher. Any kind of a blank book will do for this, except that it should not be too large to be carried in the pocket, and it should always have the pencil attached. To make the note-book a success the following rules should be observed:

(a) The book should be considered the personal property of the child and should never be criticized by the teacher except as a matter of encouragement; for the spirit in which the notes are made, is more important than the information they cover.

(b) The making of drawings should be encouraged for illustrating what is observed. A graphic drawing is far better than a long description of a natural object.

(c) The note-book should not be regarded as a part of the work in English. The spelling, language and writing of the notes should all be exempt from criticism.

(d) As occasion offers, outlines for observing certain plants or animals may be placed in the note-book previous to the field excursion so as to give definite points for the work.

(e) No child should be compelled to have a note-book.

The field note-book is a veritable gold mine for the nature-study teacher to work, in securing voluntary and happy observations from the pupils concerning their out-of-door interests. It is a friendly gate which admits the teacher to a knowledge of what the child sees and cares for. Through it she may discover where the child's attention impinges upon the realm of nature and thus may know where to find the starting point for cultivating larger intelligence and a wider interest.

I have examined many field note-books kept by pupils in the intermediate grades and have been surprised at their plenitude of accurate observation and graphic illustration. These books ranged from blank account books furnished by the family grocer up to a quarto, the pages of which were adorned with many marginal illustrations made in passionate admiration of Thompson-Seton's books and filled with carefully transcribed text, that showed the direct influence of Thoreau. These books, of whatever quality, are precious beyond price to their owners. And why not? For they represent what cannot be bought or sold, personal experience in the happy world of out-of-doors.

A page in the field note-book of a lad of fourteen who read Thoreau and admired the books of Thompson-Seton.

THE FIELD EXCURSION

MANY teachers look upon the field excursion as a precarious voyage, steered between the Scylla of hilarious seeing too much and the Charybdis of seeing nothing at all because of the zest which comes from freedom in the fields and wood. This danger can be obviated if the teacher plans the work definitely before starting, and demands certain results.

It is a mistake to think that a half day is necessary for a field lesson, since a very efficient field trip may be made during the ten or fifteen minutes at recess, if it is well planned. Certain questions and lines of investigation should be given the pupils before starting and given in such a manner as to make them

A brook in winter

thoroughly interested in discovering the facts. A certain teacher in New York State has studied all the common plants and trees in the vicinity of her school with these recess excursions and the pupils have been enthusiastic about the work.

The half hour excursion should be preceded by a talk concerning the purposes of the outing and the pupils must know that certain observations are to be made or they will not be permitted to go again. This should not be emphasized as a punishment; but they should be made to understand that a field excursion is only, naturally enough, for those who wish to see and understand outdoor life. For all field work, the teacher should make use of the field notebook which should be a part of the pupils' equipment.

PETS AS NATURE-STUDY SUBJECTS

LITTLE attention has been given to making the child understand what would be the lives of his pets if they were in their native environment; or to relating their habits and lives as wild animals. Almost any pet, if properly observed, affords an admirable opportunity for understanding the reasons why its structure and peculiar habits may have made it successful among other creatures and in other lands.

Moreover the actions and the daily life of the pet make interesting subject matter for a note-book. The lessons on the dog, rabbit and horse as given in this volume may suggest methods for such study, and with apologies that it is not better and more interesting, I have placed with the story of the squirrel a few pages from one of my own note-books regarding my experiences with "Furry." I include this record as a suggestion for the children that they should keep note-books of their pets. It will lead them to closer observation and to a better and more natural expression of their experiences.

Young guinea pig

THE CORRELATION OF NATURE-STUDY
WITH LANGUAGE WORK

NATURE-STUDY should be so much a part of the child's thought and interest that it will naturally form a thought core for other subjects quite unconsciously on his part. In fact, there is one safe rule for correlation in this case, it is legitimate and excellent training as long as the pupil does not discover that he is correlating. But there is something in human nature which revolts against doing one thing to accomplish quite another. A boy once said to me, "I'd rather never go on a field excursion than to have to write it up for English," a sentiment I sympathized with keenly; ulterior motive is sickening to the honest spirit. But if that same boy had been a member of a field class and had enjoyed all the new experiences and had witnessed the interesting things discovered on this excursion, and if later his teacher had asked him to write for her an account of some part of it, because *she wished to know what he had discovered*, the chances are that he would have written his story joyfully and with a certain pride that would have counted much for achievement in word expression.

When Mr. John Spencer, known to so many children in New York State as "Uncle John," was conducting the Junior Naturalist Clubs, the teachers allowed letters to him to count for language exercises; and the eagerness with which these letters were written should have given the teachers the key to the proper method of teaching English. Mr. Spencer requested the teachers not to correct the letters, because he wished the children to be thinking about the subject matter rather than the form of expression. But so anxious were many of the pupils to make their letters perfect, that they earnestly requested their teachers to help them write correctly, which was an ideal condition for teaching them English. Writing letters to Uncle John was such a joy to the pupils that it was used as a privilege and a reward of merit in many schools. One rural teacher reduced the percentage of tardiness to a minimum by giving the first period in the morning to the work in English which consisted of letters to Uncle John.

Why do pupils dislike writing English exercises? Simply because they are not interested in the subject they are asked to write about, and they know that the teacher is not interested in the information contained in the essay. But when they are interested in the subject and write about it to a person who is interested, the conditions are entirely changed. If the teacher, overwhelmed as she is by work and perplexities, could only keep in mind that the purpose of a language is, after all, merely to convey ideas, some of her perplexities would fade away. A conveyance naturally should be fitted for the load it is to carry, and if the pupil acquires the load first he is very likely to construct a conveyance that will be adequate. How often the conveyance is made perfect through much effort and polished through agony of spirit and the load entirely forgotten!

Nature-study lessons give much excellent subject matter for stories and essays, but these essays should never be criticized or defaced with the blue pencil. They should be read with interest by the teacher; the mistakes made in them, so transformed as to be unrecognizable, may be used for drill exercises in grammatical construction. After all, grammar and spelling are only gained by practice and there is no royal road leading to their acquirement.

THE CORRELATION OF NATURE-STUDY AND DRAWING

THE correlation of nature-study and drawing is so natural and inevitable that it needs never be revealed to the pupil. When the child is interested in studying any object, he enjoys illustrating his observations with drawings; the happy absorption of children thus engaged is a delight to witness. At its best, drawing is a perfectly natural method of self-expression. The savage and the young child, both untutored, seek to express themselves and their experiences by this means. It is only when the object to be drawn is foreign to the interest of the child that drawing is a task.

Nature-study offers the best means for bridging the gap that lies between the kindergarten child who makes drawings because he loves to and is impelled to from within, and the pupil in the grades who is obliged to draw what the teacher places before him. From making crude and often meaningless pencil strokes, which is the entertainment of the young child, the outlining of a leaf or some other simple and interesting natural object, is a normal step full of interest for the child because it is still self-expression.

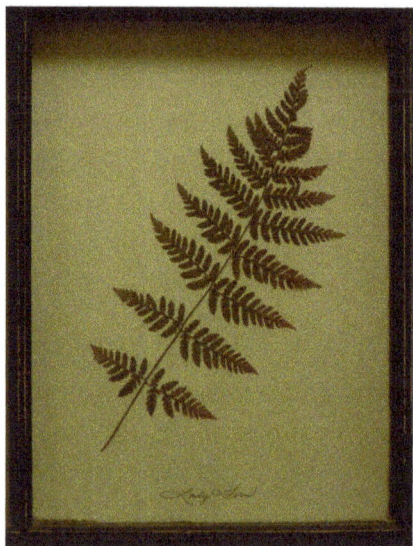

CHRIS LIGHT (CC BY-SA 4.0)
A mounted fern

Miss Mary E. Hill gives every year in the Goodyear School of Syracuse an exhibition of the drawings made by the children in the nature-study classes; and these are universally so excellent that most people regard them as an exhibition from the Art Department; and yet many of these pupils have never had lessons in drawing. They have learned to draw because they like to make pictures of the living objects which they have studied. One year there were many pictures of toads in various stages in this exhibit, and although their anatomy was sometimes awry in the pictures, yet there was a certain vivid expression of life in their representation; one felt that the toads could jump. Miss Hill allows the pupils to choose their own medium, pencil, crayon, or water-color, and says that they seem to feel which is best. For instance, when drawing the outline of trees in winter they choose pencil, but when representing the trillium or iris they prefer the water-color, while for bitter-sweet and crocuses they choose the colored crayons.

It is through this method of drawing that which interests him, that the child retains and keeps as his own, what should be an inalienable right, a graphic method of expressing his own impressions. Too much have we emphasized drawing as an art; it may be an art, if the one who draws is an artist; but if he is not an artist he still has a right to draw if it pleases him to do so. We might as well declare that a child should not speak unless he put his words into poetry, as to declare that he should not draw because his drawings are not artistic.

THE CORRELATION OF NATURE-STUDY WITH GEOGRAPHY

LIFE depends upon its environment. Geographical conditions and limitations have shaped the mold into which plastic life has been poured and by which its form has been modified. It may be easy for the untrained mind to see how the deserts and oceans affect life. Cattle may not roam in the former because there is nothing there for them to eat, nor may they occupy the latter because they are not fitted for breathing air in the water. And yet the camel can endure thirst and live on the scant food of the desert; and the whale is a mammal fitted to live in the sea. The question is, how are we to impress the child with the "have to" which lies behind all these geographical facts. If animals live in the desert they *have to* subsist on scant and peculiar food which grows there; they *have to* get along with little water; they *have to* endure heat and sand storms; they *have to* have eyes that will not become blinded by the vivid reflection of the sunlight on the sand; they *have to* be of sand color so that they may escape the eyes of their enemies or creep upon their prey unperceived.

All these have to's are not mere chance, but they have existed so long that the animal, by constantly coming in contact with them, has attained its present form and habits.

There are just as many have to's in the stream or the pond back of the school-house, on the dry hillside behind it or in the woods beyond the creek as

A meandering stream

27

there are in desert or ocean; and when the child gets an inkling of this fact, he has made a great step into the realm of geography. When he realizes why water lilies can grow only in still water that is not too deep and which has a silt bottom, and why the cat-tails grow in swamps where there is not too much water, and why the mullein grows in the dry pasture, and why the hepatica thrives in the rich, damp woods, and why the daisies grow in the meadows, he will understand that this partnership of nature and geography illustrates the laws which govern life. Many phases of physical geography belong to the realm of nature-study; the brook, its course, its work or erosion and sedimentation; the rocks of many kinds, the soil, the climate, the weather, are all legitimate subjects for nature-study lessons.

THE CORRELATION OF NATURE-STUDY WITH HISTORY

THERE are many points where nature-study impinges upon history in a way that may prove the basis for an inspiring lesson. Many of our weeds, cultivated plants and domestic animals have been introduced from Europe and are a part of our colonial history; while there are many of the most commonly seen creatures which have played their part in the history of ancient times. For instance, the bees which gave to man the only means available to him for sweetening his food until the 17th century, were closely allied to the home life of ancient peoples. The buffalo which ranged our western plains had much to do with the life of the red man. The study of the grasshopper brings to the child's attention stories of the locusts' invasion mentioned in the Bible, and the stars, which witnessed our creation and of which Job sang and the ancients wrote, shine over our heads every night.

But the trees, through the lengthy span of their lives, cover more history individually, than do other organisms. In glancing across the wood-covered hills of New York one often sees there, far above the other trees, the gaunt crowns of old white pines. Such trees belonged to the forest primeval and may have attained the age of two centuries; they stand there looking out over the world, relics of another age when America belonged to the red man, and the bear and the panther played or fought beneath them. The cedars live longer than do the pines and the great scarlet oak may have attained the age of four centuries before it yields to fate.

Perhaps in no other way may the attention of the pupil be turned so naturally to past events, as through the thought that the life of such a tree has spanned so much of human history. The life history of one of these ancient trees should be made the center of local history; let the pupils find

The treaty oak in Austin, Texas. This was once part of fourteen oak tress that served as a sacred meeting place for Comanche and Tonkawa tribes prior to European settlement.

when the town was first settled by the whites and where they came from and how large the tree was then. What Indian tribes roamed the woods before that and what animals were common in the forest when this tree was a sapling? Thus may be brought out the chief events in the history of the county and township, when they were established and for whom or what they were named; and a comparison of the present industries may be made with those of a hundred years ago.

THE CORRELATION OF NATURE-STUDY WITH ARITHMETIC

THE arithmetical problems presented by nature-study are many; some of them are simple and some of them are complicated, and all of them are illumining. Seed distribution especially lends itself to computation; a milkweed pod contains 140 seeds; there are five such pods on one plant, each milkweed plant requires at least one square foot of ground to grow on; how much ground would be required to grow all of the seeds from this one plant? Or, count the seeds in one dandelion head, multiply by the number of flower heads on the plant and estimate how many plants can grow on a square foot, then ask a boy how long it would take for one dandelion plant to cover his father's farm with its progeny; or count the blossoms on one branch of an apple tree, later count the ripened fruit; what percentage of blossoms ma-

29

BALARAM MAHALDER (CC BY-SA 2.0)
A spreading banyan tree

tured into fruit? Measuring trees, their height and thickness and computing the lumber they will make combines arithmetic and geometry, and so on *ad infinitum.*

As a matter of fact, the teacher will find in almost every nature lesson an arithmetic lesson; and when arithmetic is used in this work, it should be vital and inherent and not "tacked on;" the pupils should be really interested in the answers to their problems; and as with all correlation, the success of it depends upon the genius of the teacher.

GARDENING AND NATURE-STUDY

ERRONEOUSLY, some people maintain that gardening is nature-study; this is not so necessarily nor ordinarily. Gardening may be a basis for nature-study but it is rarely made so to any great extent. Even the work in children's gardens is so conducted that the pupils know little or nothing of the flowers or vegetables which they grow except their names, their uses to man and how to cultivate them. They are taught how to prepare the soil, but the reason for this from the plant's standpoint is never revealed; and if the child becomes acquainted with the plants in his garden, he makes the discovery by himself. All this is nothing against gardening! It is a wholesome and valuable experience for a child to learn how to make a garden even if he remains ignorant of the interesting facts concerning the plants which he there cultivates. But if the teachers are so inclined, they may find in the garden and its products, the most interesting material for the best of nature lessons. Every plant the child grows is an individual with its own peculiarities as well as those of its species in manner of growth. Its roots, stems and leaves are of certain form and structure; and often the special uses to the plant of its own kind of leaves, stems and roots are obvious. Each plant has its own form of flower and even its own tricks for securing pollenation; and its own manner of developing and scattering its seeds. Every weed of the garden has developed some special method of winning and holding its place among the cultivated plants; and in no other way may the child so fully and naturally come into a comprehension of that term "the survival of the fittest" as by studying the ways of the fit as exemplified in the triumphant weeds of his garden.

Every earthworm working below the soil is doing something for the garden. Every bee that visits the flowers there is on an errand for the garden as well as for herself. Every insect feeding on leaf or root is doing something to the garden. Every bird that nests near by or that ever visits it, is doing something which affects the life and the growth of the garden. What all of these uninvited guests are doing is one field of garden nature-study. Aside from all this study of individual life in the garden which even the youngest child may take part in, there are the more advanced lessons on the soil. What kind of soil is it? From what sort of rock was it formed? What renders it mellow and fit for the growing of plants? Moreover, what do the plants get from it? How do they get it? What do they do with what they get?

This leads to the subject of plant physiology, the elements of which may be taught simply by experiments carried on by the children themselves, experiments which should demonstrate the sap currents in the plant; the use of water to carry food and in making the plant rigid; the use of sunshine in making the plant food in the leaf laboratories; the nourishment provided for the seed and its germination, and many other similar lessons.

A child who makes a garden, and thus becomes intimate with the plants he cultivates, and comes to understand the interrelation of the various forms of life which he finds in his garden, has progressed far in the fundamental knowledge of nature's ways as well as in a practical knowledge of agriculture.

NATURE-STUDY AND AGRICULTURE

LUCKILY, thumb-rule agriculture is being pushed to the wall in these enlightened days. Thumb rules would work much better if nature did not vary her performances in such a confusing way. Government experiment stations were established because thumb rules for farming were unreliable and disappointing; and all the work of all the experiment stations has been simply advanced nature-study and its application to the practice of agriculture. Both nature-study and agriculture are based upon the study of life and the physical conditions which encourage or limit life; this is known to the world as the study of the natural sciences; and if we see clearly the relation of nature-study to science, we may understand better the relation of nature-study to agriculture, which is based upon the sciences.

Nature-study is science brought home. It is a knowledge of botany, zoology and geology as illustrated in the dooryard, the corn-field or the woods back of the house. Some people have an idea that to know these sciences one must go to college; they do not understand that nature has furnished the material and laboratories on every farm in the land. Thus, by beginning with the child in nature-study we take him to the laboratory of the wood or garden, the roadside or the field, and his materials are the wild flowers or the weeds, or the insects that visit the golden-rod or the bird that sings in the maple tree, or the woodchuck whistling in the pasture. The child begins to study living things anywhere or everywhere, and his progress is always along the various tracks laid down by the laws of life, along which his work as an agriculturist must always progress if it is to be successful.

The child through nature-study learns the way a plant grows, whether it be an oak, a turnip or a pigweed; he learns how the roots of each is adapted to its needs; how the leaves place themselves to get the sunshine and why they need it; and how the flowers get their pollen carried by the bee or wind; and how the seeds are finally scattered and planted. Or he learns about the life of the bird, whether it be a chicken, an owl or a bobolink; he knows how each bird gets its food and what its food is, where it lives, where it nests and its relation to other living things. He studies the bumblebee and discovers its great mission of pollen carrying for many flowers, and in the end would

Bales of straw

no sooner strike it dead than he would voluntarily destroy his clover patch. This is the kind of learning we call nature-study and not science or agriculture. But the country child can never learn anything in nature-study that has not something to do with science; and that has not its own practical lesson for him, when he shall become a farmer.

Some have argued, "Why not make nature-study along the lines of agriculture solely? Why should not the child begin nature-study with the cabbage rather than the wild flowers?" This argument carried out logically provides recreation for a boy in hoeing corn rather than in playing ball. Many parents in the past have argued thus and have, in consequence, driven thousands of splendid boys from the country to the city with a loathing in their souls for the drudgery which seemed all there was to farm life. The reason why the wild flowers may be selected for beginning the nature-study of plants, is because every child loves these woodland posies, and his happiest hours are spent in gathering them. Never yet have we known of a case where a child having gained his knowledge of the way a plant lives through studying the plants he loves, has failed to be interested and delighted to find that the wonderful things he discovered about his wild flower may be true of the vegetable in the garden, or the purslane which fights with it for ground to stand upon.

Some have said, "We, as farmers, care only to know what concerns our pocket-books; we wish only to study those things which we must, as farmers, cultivate or destroy. We do not care for the butterfly, but we wish to know the plum weevil; we do not care for the trillium but

Straw bales at harvest time

we are interested in the onion; we do not care for the meadow-lark but we cherish the gosling." This is an absurd argument since it is a mental impossibility for any human being to discriminate between two things when he knows or sees only one. In order to understand the important economic relations to the world of one plant or animal, it is absolutely necessary to have a wide knowledge of other plants and animals. One might as well say, "I will see the approaching cyclone, but never look at the sky; I will look at the clover but not see the dandelion; I will look for the sheriff when he comes over the hill but will not see any other team on the road."

Nature-study is an effort to make the individual use his senses instead of losing them; to train him to keep his eyes open to all things so that his powers of discrimination shall be based on wisdom. The ideal farmer is not the man who by hazard and chance succeeds; he is the man who loves his farm and all that surrounds it because he is awake to the beauty as well as to the wonders which are there; he is the man who understands as far as may be the great forces of nature which are at work around him, and therefore, he is able to make them work for him. For what is agriculture save a diversion of natural forces for the benefit of man! The farmer who knows these forces only when restricted to his paltry crops, and has no idea of their larger application, is no more efficient as a father than would a man be as an engineer who knew nothing of his engine except how to start and stop it.

In order to appreciate truly his farm, the farmer must needs begin as a child with nature-study; in order to be successful and make the farm pay, he must needs continue in nature-study; and to make his declining years happy, content, full of wide sympathies and profitable thought, he must needs conclude with nature-study; for nature-study is the alphabet of agriculture and no word in that great vocation may be spelled without it.

NATURE-STUDY CLUBS

THE organizing of a club by the pupils for the purpose of studying out-of-door life, is a great help and inspiration to the work in nature-study in the classroom. The essays and the talks before the club, prove efficient aid in English composition; and the varied interests of the members of the club, furnish new and vital material for study. A button or a badge may be designed for the club and, of course, it must have constitution and by-laws. The proceedings of the club meetings should be conducted according to parliamentary rules; but the field excursions should be entirely informal.

The meetings of the Junior Naturalists Clubs, as organized in the schools of New York State by Mr. John W. Spencer, were most impressive. The school session would be brought to a close, the teacher stepping down and taking a seat with the pupils. The president of the club, some bashful boy or slender slip of a girl, would take the chair and conduct the meeting with a dignity and efficiency worthy of a statesman. The order was perfect, the discussion much to the point. I confess to a feeling of awe when I attended these meetings, conducted so seriously and so formally, by such youngsters. Undoubtedly, the parliamentary training and experience in speaking impromptu, are among the chief benefits of such a club.

These clubs may be organized for special study. In one bird club of which I know there have been contests. Sides were chosen and the number of birds seen from May 1st to 31st inclusive was the test of supremacy. Notes on the birds were taken in the field with such care, that when at the end of the month each member handed in his notes, they could be used as evidence of accurate identification. An umpire with the help of bird manuals decided the doubtful points. This year the score stood 79 to 81.

The programs of the nature club should be varied so as to be continually interesting. Poems and stories, concerning the objects studied, help make the program attractive.

HOW TO USE THIS BOOK

FIRST and indispensably, the teacher should have at hand the subject of the lesson. She should make herself familiar with the points covered by the questions and read the story before giving the lesson. If she does not have the time to go over the observations suggested, before giving the lesson, she should take up the questions with the pupils as a joint investigation, and be boon companion in discovering the story.

The story should not be read to the pupils. It is given as an assistance to the teacher, and is not meant for direct information to the pupils. If the teacher knows a fact in nature's realm, she is then in a position to lead her pupils to discover this fact for themselves.

Make the lesson an investigation and make the pupils feel that they are investigators. To tell the story to begin with, inevitably spoils this attitude and quenches interest.

The "leading thought" embodies some of the points which should be in the teacher's mind while giving the lesson; it should not be read or declared to the pupils.

The outlines for observations herein given, by no means cover all of the observations possible; they are meant to suggest to the teacher observations of her own, rather than to be followed slavishly.

The suggestions for observations have been given in the form of questions, merely for the sake of saving space. The direct questioning method, if not employed with discretion, becomes tiresome to both pupil and teacher. If the questions do not inspire the child to investigate, they are useless. To grind out answers to questions about any natural object is not nature-study, it is simply "grind," a form of mental activity which is of much greater use when applied to spelling or the multiplication table than to the study of nature. The best teacher will cover the points suggested for observations with few direct questions. To those who find the questions inadequate I will say that, although I have used these outlines once, I am sure I should never be able to use them again without making changes.

The topics chosen for these lessons may not be the most practical nor the most interesting nor the most enlightening that are to be found; they are simply those subjects which I have used in my classes, because we happened to find them at hand the mornings the lessons were given.

While an earnest attempt has been made to make the information in this book accurate, it is to be expected and to be hoped that many discrepancies will be found by those who follow the lessons. No two animals or plants are just alike, and no two people see things exactly the same way. *The chief aim of this volume is to encourage investigation rather than to give information.* Therefore, if mistakes are found, the object of the book will have been accomplished, and the author will feel deeply gratified. If the teacher finds that the observations made by her and her pupils, do not agree with the statements in the book, I earnestly enjoin upon her to trust to her own eyes rather than to any book.

No teacher is expected to teach all the lessons in this book. A wide range of subjects is given, so that congenial choice may be made.

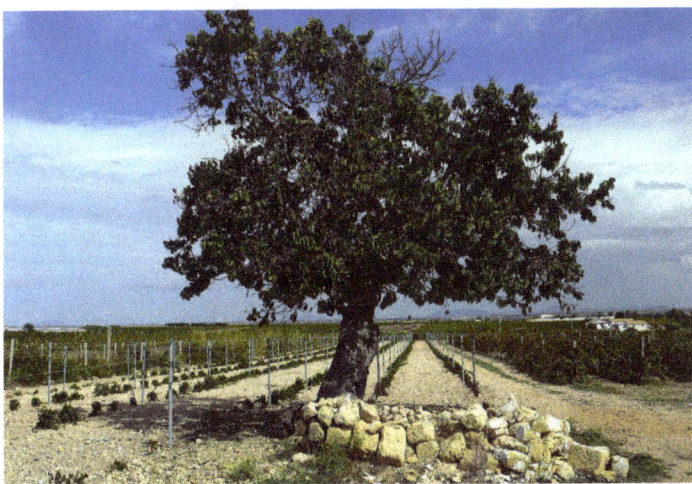

An old mulberry tree

FISH

FISH

"It remains yet unresolved whether the happiness of a man in this world doth consist more in contemplation or action. Concerning which two opinions I shall forebear to add a third by declaring my own, and rest myself contented in telling you that both of these meet together, and do most properly belong to the most honest, ingenious, quiet and harmless art of angling. And first I tell you what some have observed, and I have found to be a real truth, that the very sitting by the riverside is not only the quietest and the fittest place for contemplation, but will invite an angler to it."

—ISAAK WALTON.

DEAR, human, old Isaak Walton discovered that nature-study, fishing, and philosophy were akin and as inevitably related as the three angles of a triangle. And yet it is surprising how little the fish have been used as subjects for nature lessons. Every brook and pond is a treasure to the teacher who will find what there is in it and who knows what may be gotten out of it.

Luckily there are some very good books on fishes which will assist materially in making the fish lessons interesting: Fishes, by David Starr Jordan, is a magnificent popular work in two volumes; American Food and Game Fishes, by Jordan and Evermann, is one of the volumes of the valuable Nature Library. While for supplementary reading the following will prove instructive and entertaining: The Story of the Fishes, Baskett; Fish Stories, by Holder and Jordan; "The Story of a Salmon," in Science Sketches, by Jordan; Neighbors with Wings and Fins, Johonnot; Half Hours with Fishes, Reptiles and Birds, Holder.

Almost any of the fishes found in brook or pond may be kept in an aquarium for a few days of observation in the schoolroom. A water pail or bucket does very well if there is no glass aquarium. The water should be changed every day and at least once a day it should be aerated by dipping it up and pouring it back from some distance above. The practice should be established, once for all, of putting these finny prisoners back into the brook after they have been studied.

The Goldfish

TEACHER'S STORY

ONCE upon a time, if stories are true, there lived a king called Midas, whose touch turned everything to gold. Whenever I see goldfish, I wonder if, perhaps, King Midas were not a Chinese and if he perchance did not handle some of the little fish in Orient streams. But common man has learned a magic as wonderful as that of King Midas, although it does not act so immediately, for it is through his agency in selecting and breeding that we have gained these exquisite fish for our aquaria. In the streams of China the goldfish, which were the ancestors of these effulgent creatures, wore safe green colors like the shiners in our brooks; and if any goldfish escape from our fountains and run wild, their progeny return to their native olive-green color. There are many such dull-colored goldfish in the Delaware and Potomac and other eastern rivers. It is almost inconceivable that one of the brilliant colored fishes, if it chanced to escape into our ponds, should escape the fate of being eaten by some larger fish attracted by such glittering bait.

DB THATS-ME (CC BY-SA 3.0)
Feeding the fish at a trout hatchery

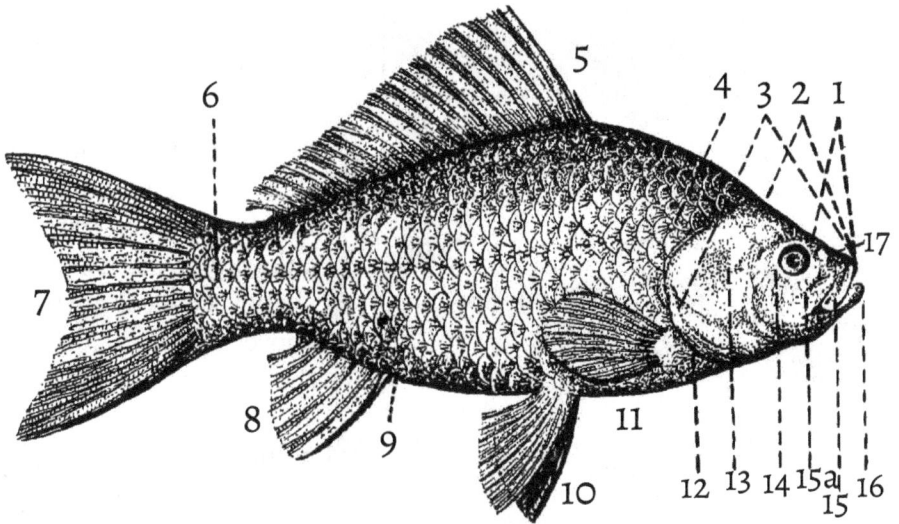

PARTS OF A GOLDFISH

1. Snout	2. Distance from snout to nape	3. Head
4. Lateral line	5. Dorsal fin 6. Base of caudal fin	7. Caudal fin
8. Anal fin 9. Anus	10. Ventral fin	11. Pectoral fin
12. Branchiostegals	13. Operculum	14. Eye
15a. Preorbital 15. Upper jaw	16. Lower jaw	17. Nostril

The goldfish, as we see it in the aquarium, is brilliant orange above and pale lemon-yellow below; there are many specimens that are adorned with black patches. And as if this fish were bound to imitate the precious metals, there are individuals which are silver instead of gold: they are oxidized silver above and polished silver below. The goldfish are closely related to the carp and can live in waters that are stale. However, the water in the aquarium should be changed at least twice a week to keep it clear. Goldfish should not be fed too lavishly. An inch square of one of the sheets of prepared fish food, we have found a fair daily ration for five medium sized fish; these fish are more likely to die from overfeeding than from starving. Goldfish are naturally long-lived; Miss Ada Georgia has kept them until seven years old in a school aquarium; and there is on record one goldfish that lived nine years.

Too often the wonderful common things are never noticed because of their commonness; and there is no better instance of this than the form and movements of a fish. It is an animal in many ways similar to animals that live on land; but its form and structure are such that it is

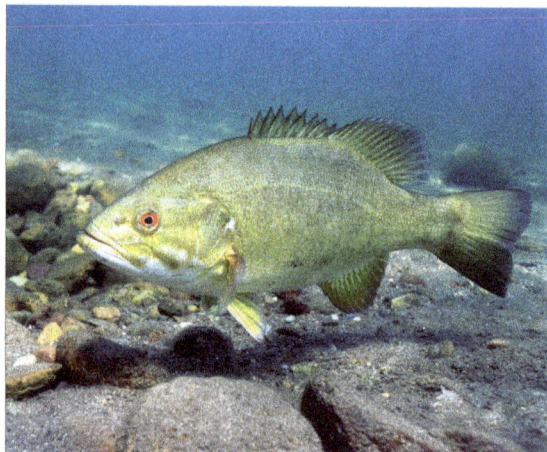
Smallmouth Bass
Micropterus dolomieu

perfectly adapted to live in water all its life; there are none of the true fishes which live portions of their lives on land as do the frogs. The first peculiarity of the fish is its shape. Looked at from above, the broader part of the body is near the front end which is rounded or pointed so as to cut the water readily. The long, narrow, hind portion of the body with the tail acts as a propeller. Seen from the side, the body is a smooth, graceful oval and this form is especially adapted to move through the water swiftly, as can be demonstrated to the pupil by cutting a model of the fish from wood and trying to move it through the water sidewise.

Normally, the fish has seven fins, one along the back called the dorsal, one at the end of the tail called the tail or caudal fin, one beneath the rear end of the body called the anal, a pair on the lower side of the body called the ventrals, and a pair just back of the gill openings called the pectorals. All these fins play their own parts in the movements of the fish. The dorsal fin is usually higher in front than behind and can be lifted or shut down like a fan. This fin when it is lifted gives the fish greater height and it can be twisted to one side or the other and thus be made a factor in steering. The anal fin on the lower side acts in a similar manner. The tail fin is the propeller and sends the body forward by pressing backward on the water, first on one side and then on the other, being used like a scull. The tail fin varies in shape very much in different species. In the goldfish it is fanlike, with a deeply notched hind edge, but in some it is rounded or square.

The paired fins correspond anatomically to our arms and legs, the pectorals representing the arms, the ventrals the legs. Fins are made up of rays, as the bony rods are called which support the membrane;

these rays are of two kinds, those which are soft, flexible, many jointed and usually branched at the tip; and those which are bony, not jointed and which are usually stiff spines. When the spines are present in a fin they precede the soft rays.

Fishes' eyes have no eyelid but the eyeball is movable, and this often gives the impression that the fish winks. Fishes are necessarily near-sighted since the lens of the eye has to be spherical in order to see in the water. The sense of smell is located in a little sac to which the nostril leads; the nostrils are small and often partitioned and may be seen on either side of the snout. The nostrils have no connection whatever with breathing, in the fish.

A chain pickerel
Esox niger

The tongue of the fish is very bony or bristly and immovable. There is very little sense of taste developed in it. The shape, number and position of the teeth vary according to the food habits of the fish. The commonest type of teeth are fine, sharp and short and are arranged in pads, as seen in the bullhead. Some fish have blunt teeth suitable for crushing shells. Herbivorous fishes have sharp teeth with serrated edges, while those living upon crabs and snails have incisor-like teeth. In some specimens we find several types of teeth, in others the teeth may be entirely absent. The teeth are borne not only on the jaws but also in the roof of the mouth, on the tongue and in the throat.

A yellow perch
Perca flavescens

The ear of the fish has neither outside form nor opening and is very imperfect in comparison with that of man. Extending along the sides of the body from head to tail is a line of modified scales containing small tubes connecting with nerves; this is called the lateral line and it is believed that it is in some way connected with the fish's senses, perhaps with the sense of hearing.

Since fishes must push through water, which is more difficult than moving through air, they need to have the body well protected. This protection is, in most fishes, in the form of an armor of scales which are smooth and allow the body to pass through the water with little friction. These scales overlap like shingles in a roof and are all directed backward. The study of the fish scale shows that it grows in layers.

In order to understand how the fish breathes we must examine its gills. In front, just above the entrance to the gullet, are several bony ridges which bear two rows of pinkish fringes; these are the gill arches and the fringes are the gills. The gills are filled with tiny blood vessels, and as the water passes over them, the impurities of the blood pass out through the thin skin of the gills and the life-giving oxygen passes in. Since fish cannot make use of air unless it is dissolved in water, it is very important that the water in the aquarium jar should often be replenished. The gill arches also bear a series of bony processes called gill-rakers. Their function is to prevent the escape of food through the gills while it is being swallowed, and they vary in size according to the food habits of the fish. We note that the fish in the aquarium constantly opens and closes the mouth; this action draws the water into the throat and forces it out over the gills and through the gill openings; this then, is the act of breathing.

LESSON

LEADING THOUGHT—A fish lives in the water where it must breathe, move and find its food. The water world is quite different from the air world and the fish have developed forms, senses and habits which fit them for life in the water.

METHOD—The goldfish is used as a subject for this lesson because it is so conveniently kept where the children may see it. However, a shiner or minnow would do as well.

Before the pupils begin the study, place the diagram on the blackboard, with all the parts labelled; thus the pupils will be able to learn the parts of the fish by consulting it, and not be compelled to commit them to memory arbitrarily. It would be well to associate the goldfish with a geography lesson on China.

OBSERVATIONS—

1. Where do fishes live? Do any fishes ever live any part of their lives on land like the frogs? Could a salt-water fish live in fresh water, or vice versa?

2. What is the shape of a fish when seen from above? Where is the widest part? What is its shape seen from the side? Think if you can in how many ways the shape of the fish is adapted for moving swiftly through the water.

3. How many fins has the fish? Make a sketch of the goldfish with all its fins and name them from the diagram on the blackboard.

4. How many fins are there in all? Four of these fins are in pairs; where are they situated? What are they called? Which pair corresponds to our arms? Which to our legs?

5. Describe the pectoral fins. How are they used? Are they kept constantly moving? Do they move together or alternately? How are they used when the fish swims backwards?

6. How are the ventral fins used? How do they assist the fish when swimming?

7. Sketch a dorsal fin. How many spines has it? How many soft rays are there in it? What is the difference in structure between the stiff spines in the front of the dorsal fin and the rays in the hind portion? Of what use to the fish are these two different kinds of fin supports?

8. Sketch the anal fin. Has it any spines in front? How many rays has it? How is this fin used when the fish is swimming?

9. With what fin does the fish push itself through the water? Make a sketch of the tail. Note if it is square, rounded, or notched at the end. Are the rays of the tail fin spiny or soft in character?

10. Watch the goldfish swim and describe the action of all the fins while it is in motion. In what position are the fins when the fish is at rest?

11. What is the nature of the covering of the fish? Are the scales large or small? In which direction do they seem to overlap? Of what use to the fish is this scaly covering?

12. Can you see a line which extends from the upper part of the gill opening, along the side to the tail? This is called the lateral line. Do you think it is of any use to the fish?

13. Note carefully the eyes of the fish. Describe the pupil and the iris. Are the eyes placed so that the fish can see in all directions? Can they be moved so as to see better in any direction? Does the fish wink? Has it any eyelids? Do you know why fish are near-sighted?

14. Can you see the nostrils? Is there a little wart-like projection connected with the nostril? Do you think fishes breathe through their nostrils?

15. Describe the mouth of the fish. Does it open upward, downward, or directly in front? What sort of teeth have fish? How does the fish catch its prey? Does the lower or upper jaw move in the process of eating?

16. Is the mouth kept always in motion? Do you think the fish is swallowing water all the time? Do you know why it does this? Can you see a wide opening along the sides of the head behind the gill cover? Does the gill cover move with the movement of the mouth? How does a fish breathe?

17. What are the colors of the goldfish above and below? What would happen to our beautiful goldfish if they were put in a brook with other fish? Why could they not hide? Do you know what happens to the colors of the goldfish when they run wild in our streams and ponds?

18. Can you find in books or cyclopedias where the goldfish came from? Are they gold and silver in color in the streams where they are native? Do you think that they had originally the long, slender, swal-

low tails which we see sometimes in goldfish? How have the beautiful colors and graceful forms of the gold and silver fishes been developed?

"I have my world, and so have you,
A tiny universe for two,
A bubble by the artist blown,
Scarcely more fragile than our own,
Where you have all a whale could wish,
Happy as Eden's primal fish.
Manna is dropt you thrice a day
From some kind heaven not far away,
And still you snatch its softening crumbs,
Nor, more than we, think whence it comes.
No toil seems yours but to explore
Your cloistered realm from shore to shore;
Sometimes you trace its limits round,
Sometimes its limpid depths you sound,
Or hover motionless midway,
Like gold-red clouds at set of day;
Erelong you whirl with sudden whim
Off to your globe's most distant rim,
Where, greatened by the watery lens,
Methinks no dragon of the fens
Flashed huger scales against the sky,
Roused by Sir Bevis or Sir Guy;
And the one eye that meets my view,
Lidless and strangely largening, too,
Like that of conscience in the dark,
Seems to make me its single mark.
What a benignant lot is yours
That have an own All-out-of-doors,
No words to spell, no sums to do,
No Nepos and no parlyvoo!
How happy you, without a thought
Of such cross things as Must and Ought—
I too the happiest of boys
To see and share your golden joys!"

—"THE ORACLE OF THE GOLDFISHES," LOWELL.

Common bullhead
Ameiurus nebulosus

The Bullhead

TEACHER'S STORY

"The bull-head does usually dwell and hide himself in holes or amongst stones in clear water; and in very hot days will lie a long time very still and sun himself and will be easy to be seen on any flat stone or gravel; at which time he will suffer an angler to put a hook baited with a small worm very near into his mouth; and he never refuses to bite, nor indeed, to be caught with the worst of anglers."
—ISAAK WALTON.

WHEN one looks a bullhead in the face one is glad that it is not a real bull for its barbels give it an appearance quite fit for the making of a nightmare; and yet from the standpoint of the bullhead, how truly beautiful those fleshy feelers are! For without them how could it feel its way about searching for food in the mud where it lives? Two of these barbels stand straight up; the two largest ones stand out on each side of the mouth, and two pairs of short ones adorn the lower lip, the smallest pair at the middle.

As the fish moves about, it is easy to see that the large barbels at the side of the mouth are of the greatest use; it keeps them in a constantly advancing movement, feeling of everything it meets. The upper ones stand straight up, keeping watch for whatever news there may be from above; the two lower ones spread apart and follow rather than precede the fish, seeming to test what lies below. The upper and lower pairs seem to test things as they are, while the large side pair deal with what is going to be. The broad mouth seems to be formed for taking in all things eatable, for the bullhead lives on almost anything alive or

50

dead that it discovers as it noses about in the mud. Nevertheless, it has its notions about its food for I have repeatedly seen one draw material into its mouth through its breathing motion and then spew it out with a vehemence one would hardly expect from such a phlegmatic fish.

Although it has feelers which are very efficient, it also has perfectly good eyes which it uses to excellent purpose; note how promptly it moves to the other side of the aquarium when we are trying to study it. The eyes are not large; the pupils are black and oval and are rimmed with a narrow band of shiny pale yellow. The eyes are prominent so that when moved backward and forward they gain a view of the enemy in the rear or at the front while the head is motionless. It seems strange to see such a pair of pale yellow, almost white eyes in such a dark body.

The general shape of the front part of the body is flat, in fact, it is decidedly like a tadpole; this shape is especially fitted for groping about muddy bottoms. The flat effect of the body is emphasized by the gill covers opening below rather than at the sides, every pulsation widening the broad neck. The pectoral fins also open out on the same plane as the body although they can be turned at an angle if necessary; they are thick and fleshy and the sharp tips of their spines offer punishment to whosoever touches them. The dorsal fin is far forward and not large; it is usually raised at a threatening angle.

There is a little fleshy dorsal fin near the tail which stands in line with the body and one wonders what is its special use. The ventral fins are small. The anal fin is far back and rather strong, and this with the long, strong tail gives the fish good motor power and it can swim very rapidly if occasion requires.

The bullhead is mud-colored and has no scales; and since it lives in the mud, it does not need scales to protect it; but because of its scaleless condition it is a constant victim of the lampreys, and it would do well, indeed, if it could develop an armor of scales against this parasite. The skin is very thick and leathery so that it is always removed before the fish is cooked. The bullhead is the earliest fish of the spring. This is probably because it burrows deep into the mud in the fall and remains there all winter; when the spring freshets come, it emerges and is hungry for fresh meat.

The family life of the bullheads and other catfishes seems to be quite ideal. Dr. Theodore Gill tells us that bullheads make their nests by removing stones and gravel from a more or less irregularly circular area in shallow water, and on sandy or gravelly ground. The nest is somewhat excavated, both parents removing the pebbles by sucking them into the mouth and carrying them off for some distance. After the eggs are laid, the male watches over and guards the nest and seems to have great family responsibilities. He is the more active of the two in stirring and mixing the young fry after they are hatched. Smith and Harron describe the process thus: "With their chins on the bottom, the old fish brush the corners where the fry were banked, and with the barbels all directed forward, and flexed where they touch the bottom, thoroughly agitate the mass of fry, bringing the deepest individuals to the surface. This act is usually repeated several times in quick succession."

"The nests are usually made beneath logs or other protecting objects and in shallow water. The paternal care is continued for many days after the birth of the young. At first these may be crowded together in a dense mass, but as time passes they disperse more and more and spread around the father. Frequently, especially when the old one is feeding, some—one or more—of the young are taken into the mouth, but they are instinctively separated from the food and spit out. At last the young swarm venture farther from their birthplace, or perhaps they are led away by their parents."

LESSON

LEADING THOUGHT— The bullhead lives in mud bottoms of streams and ponds and is particularly adapted for life in such locations.

METHOD— A small bullhead may be placed in a small aquarium jar. At first let the water be clear and add a little pond weed so as to observe the natural tendency of the fish to hide. Later add mud and gravel to the aquarium and note the behavior of the fish.

OBSERVATIONS—

1. What at the first glance distinguishes the bullhead from other fish? Describe these strange "whiskers" growing about the mouth;

how many are there and where are they situated? Which are the longest pair? Can the fish move them in any direction at will?

2. Where do we find bullheads? On what do they feed? Would their eyes help them to find their food in the mud? How do they find it?

3. Explain, if you can, why the bullhead has barbels, or feelers, while the trout and bass have none.

4. What is the shape of the bullhead's mouth?

5. What is the general shape of the body? What is its color? Has it any scales?

6. Why should the bullhead be so flat horizontally while the sunfish is so flat in the opposite direction?

7. Describe the bullhead's eyes. Are they large? What is their color? Where are they placed?

8. Describe the dorsal fin, giving its comparative size and position. Do you see another dorsal fin? Where is this peculiar fin and how does it differ from the others?

9. Describe the tail fin. Does it seem long and strong? Is the bullhead a good swimmer?

10. Is the anal fin large or small as compared with that of the goldfish?

11. How do the pectoral fins move as compared with those of the sunfish? Why is the position of the pectoral and dorsal fins of benefit to this fish?

12. How does the bullhead inflict wounds when it is handled? Tell how these spines protect it from its natural enemies.

13. When is the best season for fishing for bullheads? Does the place where they are found affect the flavor of their flesh? Why?

14. What is the spawning season? Do you know about the nests the bullheads build and the care they give their young?

15. Write an essay on the nest-making habits of the bullheads and the care given the young by the parents.

"And what fish will the natural boy naturally take? In America, there is but one fish which enters fully into the spirit of the occasion. It is a fish of many species according to the part of the country, and of as many sizes as there are sizes of boys. This fish is the horned pout, and all the rest of the species of Ameiurus.

Horned pout is its Boston name. Bullhead is good enough for New York; and for the rest of the country, big and little, all the fishes of this tribe are called catfish. A catfish is a jolly blundering sort of a fish, a regular Falstaff of the ponds. It has a fat jowl, and a fat belly, which it is always trying to fill. Smooth and sleek, its skin is almost human in its delicacy. It wears a long mustache, with scattering whiskers of other sort. Meanwhile it always goes armed with a sword, three swords, and these it has always on hand, always ready for a struggle on land as well as in the water. The small boy often gets badly stuck on these poisoned daggers, but, as the fish knows how to set them by a muscular twist, the small boy learns how, by a like untwist, he may unset and leave them harmless.

The catfish lives in sluggish waters. It loves the millpond best of all, and it has no foolish dread of hooks when it goes forth to bite. Its mouth is wide. It swallows the hook, and very soon it is in the air, its white throat gasping in the untried element. Soon it joins its fellows on the forked stick, and even then, uncomfortable as it may find its new relations, it never loses sight of the humor of the occasion. Its large head and expansive forehead betoken a large mind. It is the only fish whose brain contains a Sylvian fissure, a piling up of tissue consequent on the abundance of gray matter. So it understands and makes no complaint. After it has dried in the sun for an hour, pour a little water over its gills, and it will wag its tail, and squeak with gratitude. And the best of all is, there are horned pouts enough to go around."

"The female horned pout lays thousands of eggs, and when these hatch, she goes about near the shore with her school of little fishes, like a hen with myriad chicks. She should be respected and let alone, for on her success in rearing this breed of 'bullying little rangers' depends the sport of the small boy of the future."

—DAVID STARR JORDAN, IN FISH STORIES.

The common sucker
Catostomus commersonnii

The Common Sucker

TEACHER'S STORY

HE who loves to peer down into the depths of still waters, often sees upon the sandy, muddy or rocky bottom several long, wedge-shaped sticks lying at various angles one to another. But if he thrust down a real stick, behold, these inert, water-logged sticks move off deftly! And then he knows that they are suckers. He may drop a hook baited with a worm in front of the nose of one, and if he waits long enough before he pulls up he may catch this fish, not by its gills but by the pit of its stomach; for it not only swallows the hook completely but tries to digest it along with the worm. Its food is made up of soft-bodied insects and other small water creatures; it is also a mud eater and manages to make a digestive selection from the organic material of silt. For this latter reason, it is not a desirable food fish although its flesh varies in flavor with the locality where it is found. The suckers taken along the rocky shores of Cayuga Lake are fairly palatable, while those taken in the mud of the Cayuga Inlet are very inferior in flavor and often uneatable.

Seen from above, the sucker is wedge-shaped, being widest at the eyes; seen from the side it has a flat lower surface and an ungracefully rounded contour above which tapers only slightly toward the tail. The profile of the face gives the impression of a Roman nose. The young specimens have an irregular scale-mosaic pattern of olive-green blotches on a paler ground color, while the old ones are quite brown above and on the sides. The suckers differ from most other fishes in having the markings of the back extend down the sides almost to the belly. This is a help in concealing the fish, since its sides show from above quite as distinctly as its back because of its peculiar form. The scales are rather large and are noticeably larger behind than in the region of the head. Like other fish it is white below.

The dorsal fin is placed about midway the length of the fish as measured from nose to tail. It is not large and appears to have twelve rays; but there is a short spine in front and a delicate soft ray behind so that it really has fourteen. The tail is long and strong and deeply notched: the anal fin extends back to where the tail begins. The ventral fins are small and are directly opposite the hind half of the dorsal fin. The pectorals are not large but are strong and are placed low down. The sucker has not a lavish equipment of fins but its tail is strong and it can swim swiftly; it is also a tremendous jumper; it will jump from the aquarium more successfully than any other fish. When resting on the bottom, it is supported by its extended pectoral and ventral fins, which are strong although not large.

The eyes are fairly large but the iris is not shiny; they are placed so that the fish can easily see above it as well as at the sides; the eyes move so as to look up or down and are very well adapted to serve a fish that lives upon the bottom. The nostrils are divided, the partition project-ing until it seems a tubercle on the face. The mouth opens below and looks like the puckered opening of a bag. The lips are thick but are very sensitive; it is by projecting these lips, in a way that reminds one of a very short elephant's trunk, that it is enabled to reach and find its food in the mud or gravel; so although the sucker's mouth is not a beautiful feature, it is doubly useful. The sucker has the habit of remaining mo-tionless for long periods of time. It breathes very slowly and appears sluggish; it never seizes its food with any spirit but simply slowly engulfs it; and for this reason it is considered poor game. It is only in the spring when they may be speared through the ice that there is any fun in catching suckers; it is at this season of the year that they move to shallow water to spawn; those in the lakes move to the rivers, those in the rivers to the creeks, those in the creeks to the brooks. Even so lowly a creature as the sucker seems to respond to influences of the springtime, for at that period the male has a faint rosy stripe along his sides. In the winter these fish burrow in the mud of the river or pond bottoms; they may be frozen and thawed without harming them.

There are many species of suckers and they vary in size from six inches to three feet in length. They inhabit all sorts of waters, but they do not like a strong current and are, therefore, found in still pools. The common sucker (*Catostomus commersoni*), which is the subject of this lesson, sometimes attains the length of twenty-two inches and the weight of five pounds. The ones under observation were about eight inches long, and proved to be the acrobats of the aquarium, since they were likely at any moment to jump out; several times I found one languishing on the floor.

LESSON

LEADING THOUGHT— The sucker is especially adapted by shape for lying on the bottom of ponds under still water where its food is abundant.

METHOD— If still water pools along river or lakesides are accessible, it is far more interesting to study a sucker in its native haunts, as an introduction to the study of its form and colors when it is in the aquarium.

OBSERVATIONS—

1. Where do you find suckers? How do you catch them? Do they take the hook quickly? What is the natural food of the sucker?

2. What is the shape of this fish's body when seen from above? From the side? What is the color above? On the sides? Below? Does the sucker differ from most other fishes in the coloring along its sides? What is the reason for this? What do suckers look like on the bottom of the pond? Are they easily seen?

3. Describe or sketch a sucker, showing the position, size and shape of the fins and tail. Are its scales large or small? How does it use its fins when at rest? When moving? Is it a strong swimmer? Is it a high jumper?

4. Describe the eyes; how are they especially adapted in position and in movement to the needs of a fish that lives on the bottom of streams and ponds?

5. Note the nostrils; what is there peculiar about them?

6. Where is the mouth of the sucker situated? What is its form? How is it adapted to get the food which the sucker likes best?

7. Tell all you know about the habits of the suckers. When do you see them first in the spring? Where do they spend the winter? Where do they go to spawn? How large is the largest one you have ever seen? Why is their flesh usually considered poor in quality as food? Is there a difference in the flavor of its flesh depending upon the locality in which the fish lives? Why?

Common shiner or redfin
Notropis cornutus

The Shiner

TEACHER'S STORY

"This is a noteworthy and characteristic lineament, or cipher, or hieroglyphic, or type of spring. You look into some clear, sandy bottomed brook where it spreads into a deeper bay, yet flowing cold from ice and snow not far off, and see indistinctly poised over the sand on invisible fins, the outlines of the shiner, scarcely to be distinguished from the sands behind it as if it were transparent."

—THOREAU.

THERE are many species of shiners and it is by no means easy to recognize them nor to distinguish them from chub, dace and minnows since all these belong to one family; they all have the same arrangement of fins and live in the same water; and the plan of this lesson can with few changes be applied to any of them.

Never were seen more exquisite colors than shimmer along the sides of the common shiner (*Notropis cornutus*). It is pale olive-green above, just a sunny brook-color; this is bordered at the sides by a line of iridescent blue-purple, while the shining silver scales on the sides below, flash and glimmer with the changing hues of the rainbow. The minnows are darker than the shiners; the horned dace develops little tubercles on the head during the breeding season, which are lost later.

The body of the shiner is ideal for slipping through the water. Seen from above it is a narrow wedge, rounded in front and tapering to a point behind; from the side, it is long, oval, lance-shaped. The scales are large and beautiful, the lateral line looks like a series of dots embroidered at the center of the diamond-shaped scales.

The dorsal fin is placed just back of the center of the body and is not very large; it is composed of soft rays, the first two being stiff and unbranched. The tail is long, large, graceful and deeply notched. The anal fin is almost as large as the dorsal. The ventral pair is placed on the lower side, opposite the dorsal fin; the pectorals are set at the lower margin of the body, just behind the gill openings. The shiner and its relatives use the pectoral fins to aid in swimming, and keep them constantly in motion when moving through the water. The ventrals are moved only now and then and evidently help in keeping the balance. When the fish moves rapidly forward, the dorsal fin is raised so that its front edge stands at right angles to the body and the ventral and anal fins are expanded to their fullest extent. But when the fish is lounging, the dorsal, anal and ventral fins are more or less closed, although the tip of the dorsal fin swings with every movement of the fish.

The eyes are large, the pupils being very large and black; the iris is pale yellow and shining; the whole eye is capable of much movement forward and back. The nostril is divided by a little projecting partition which looks like a tubercle. The mouth is at the front of the head; to see the capabilities of this mouth, watch the shiner yawn, if the water of the aquarium becomes stale. Poor fellow! He yawns just as we do in the effort to get more oxygen.

The shiners are essentially brook fish although they may be found in larger bodies of water. They lead a precarious existence, for the larger fish eat them in all their stages. They only hold their own by laying countless numbers of eggs. They feed on water insects and get even with their big fish enemies by eating their eggs. They are pretty and graceful little creatures and may be seen swimming up the current in the middle of the brook. They often occur in schools or flocks, especially when young.

LESSON

LEADING THOUGHT— The shiners are among the most common of the little fish in our small streams. They are beautiful in form and play an important part in the life of our streams.

METHOD— Place in the aquarium shiners and as many as possible of the other species of small fish found in our creeks and brooks. The aquarium should stand where the pupil may see it often. The following questions may be asked, giving the children plenty of time for the work of observation.

OBSERVATIONS—

1. Do you know how the shiner differs in appearance from the minnow and chub and dace?

2. What is the shape of the shiner's body when seen from above? When seen from the side? Do you think that its shape fits it for moving rapidly through the water?

3. What is the coloring above? On the sides? Below?

4. Are the scales large and distinct, or very small? Can you see the lateral line? Where are the tiny holes, which make this line, placed in the scales?

5. Describe or sketch the fish, showing position, relative size and shape of all the fins and the tail.

6. Describe the use and movements of each of the fins when the fish is swimming.

7. Describe the eyes. Do they move?

8. Describe the nostrils. Do you think each one is double?

9. Does the mouth open upwards, downwards or forwards? Have you ever seen the shiner yawn? Why does it yawn? Why do you yawn?

10. Where do you find the shiners living? Do they haunt the middle of the stream or the edges? Do you ever see them in flocks or schools?

MINNOWS

How silent comes the water round that bend;
Not the minutest whisper does it send
To the o'er hanging sallows; blades of grass
Slowly across the chequer'd shadows pass,
Why, you might read two sonnets, ere they reach
To where the hurrying freshnesses aye preach
A natural sermon o'er their pebbly beds;
Where swarms of minnows show their little heads,

Staying their wavy bodies 'gainst the streams,
To taste the luxury of sunny beams
Tempered with coolness. How they ever wrestle
With their own sweet delight, and ever nestle
Their silver bellies on the pebbly sand!
If you but scantily hold out the hand,
That very instant not one will remain;
But turn your eye, and there they are again.
The ripples seem right glad to reach those cresses,
And cool themselves among the em'rald tresses;
The while they cool themselves, they freshness give,
And moisture, that the bowery green may live.

—JOHN KEATS.

The brook trout
Salvelinus fontinalis

The Brook Trout

TEACHER'S STORY

"Up and down the brook I ran,
where beneath the banks so steep,
Lie the spotted trout asleep."

—WHITTIER.

BUT they were probably not asleep as Mr. Whittier might have observed if he had cast a fly near one of them. There is in the very haunts of the trout, a suggestion of where it gets its vigor and wariness: The cold, clear streams where the water is pure; brooks that wind in and out over rocky and pebbly beds, here shaded by trees and there dashing through the open,—it makes us feel vigorous even to think of such streams. Under the overhanging bank or in the shade of some fallen log or shelving rock, the brook trout hides where he may see all that goes on in the world above and around him without being himself seen. Woe to the unfortunate insect that falls upon the surface of the water in his vicinity or even that flies low over the surface for the trout will jump easily far out of the water to seize its prey! It is this habit of taking the insect upon and above the water's surface which has made trout fly-fishing the sport that it is. Man's ingenuity is fairly matched against the trout's cunning in this contest. I know of one old trout that has kept fishermen in the region around on the *qui vive* for years; and up to date he is still alive, making a dash now and then at a tempting bait, showing himself enough to tantalize his would-be captors with his splendid size, but always retiring at the sight of the line.

The brook trout varies much in color, depending upon the soil and the rocks of the streams in which it lives. Its back is marbled with dark olive or black, making it just the color of shaded water. This marbled coloration also marks the dorsal and the tail fins. The sides, which vary much in color, are marked with beautiful vermilion spots, each placed in the center of a larger, brownish spot. In some instances the lower surface is reddish, in others whitish. All the fins on the lower side of the body have the front edges creamy or yellowish white, with a darker streak behind.

Baby trout resting in a stream in Yosemite. When resting on a stream bed trout face into the current

The trout's head is quite large and somewhat blunt. The large eye is a little in front of the middle of the head. The dorsal fin is at about the middle of the body, and when raised is squarish in outline. Behind the dorsal fin, and near to the tail is the little, fleshy adipose fin, so called because it has no rays. The tail is fan-shaped, slightly notched at the end and is large and strong. The anal fin is rather large, being shaped much like the dorsal fin, only slightly smaller. The ventral fins are directly below the dorsal fin and a little behind its middle. The pectorals are low down, being below and just behind the gill arches.

In size the brook trout seldom is longer than seven or eight inches, but in the rivers of the Northeastern United States specimens weighing from six to eleven pounds are sometimes taken. It does not flourish in water which is warmer than 68°, but prefers a temperature of about 50°. It must have the pure water of mountain streams and cannot endure water of rivers which is polluted by mills or the refuse of cities. Where it has access to streams that flow into the ocean, it forms the salt water habit, going out to sea and remaining there during the winter. Such specimens become very large.

Where the trout live

The trout can lay eggs when about six inches in length. The eggs are laid from September until late November, although, as Mr. Bream says, the brook trout are spawned at some locality in almost every month of the year except mid-summer. One mother trout lays from 400 to 600 eggs, but the large-sized ones lay more. The period of hatching depends upon the temperature of the water. In depositing their eggs the trout seek water with gravelly bottom, often where some mountain brook opens into a larger stream. The nest is shaped by the tail of the fish, the larger stones being carried away in the mouth. To make the precious eggs secure they are covered with gravel.

There have been strict laws enacted by almost all of our states with a view to protecting the brook trout and preserving it in our streams. The open season in New York is from the 15th of April to the 1st of September, and it is illegal to take from a stream a fish that is less than five inches in length. It is the duty of every decent citizen to abide by these laws and to see to it that his neighbors observe them. The teacher cannot emphasize enough upon the child the moral value of being law-abiding. There should be in every school in the Union children's clubs which should have for their purpose civic honesty and the enforcement of laws which affect the city, village or township.

Almost any stream with suitable water may be stocked with trout from the national or the state hatcheries, but what is the use of this expense if the game laws are not observed and these fish are caught before they reach maturity, as is so often the case?

References— American Food and Game Fishes, Jordan and Evermann; Guide to American Fishes, Jordan.

LESSON

LEADING THOUGHT— The brook trout have been exterminated in our streams largely because the game laws have not been observed. The trout is the most cunning and beautiful of our common fishes and the most valuable for food. If properly guarded, every pure mountain stream in our country, could be well stocked with the brook trout.

METHOD— A trout may be kept in an aquarium of flowing water indefinitely and should be fed upon liver and hard clams chopped. If there is no aquarium with running water, the trout may be kept in an ordinary jar long enough for this lesson. The object of this lesson should be not only the study of the habits of the fish, but also a lesson in its preservation.

OBSERVATIONS—

1. In what streams are the brook trout found? Must the water be warm or cold? Can the trout live in impure water? Can it live in salt water?

2. Do the trout swim about in schools or do they live solitary? Where do they like to hide?

3. With what kind of bait is trout caught? Why does it afford such excellent sport for fly-fishing? Can you tell what the food of the trout is?

4. What is the color of the trout above? What colors along its sides? What markings make the fish so beautiful? What is its color below? Has the trout scales? Do you see the lateral line?

5. What is the general shape of the brook trout? Describe the shape, position and color of the dorsal fin. Describe the little fin behind the dorsal. Why is it unlike the other fins? What is the shape of the tail fin? Is it rounded, square or crescent-shaped across the end? What is the position and size of the anal fin compared with the dorsal? What colors on the ventral fins and where are they placed in relation to the dorsal fin? What color are the pectoral fins and how are they placed in relation to the gill arches?

6. Describe the trout's eyes. Are they large and alert? Do you think the trout is keen-sighted?

7. When and where are the eggs laid? Describe how the nest is

made. How are the eggs covered and protected?

8. Why are there no trout in the streams of your neighborhood? Could a trout live in these streams? Can you get state aid in stocking the streams?

9. What are the game laws concerning trout fishing? When is the open season? How long must the trout be to be taken legally? If you are a good citizen what do you do about the game laws?

10. Write a story telling all you know about the wariness, cunning and strength of the brook trout.

Supplementary reading— The following from Fish Stories by Holder and Jordan: "The Trout of Los Laurelles;" "The Golden Trout of the High Sierras;" "The Lure of the Rainbow." "The Story of the Salmon" in Science Sketches, "The Master of the Golden Pool" in Watchers of the Trails; The Story of the Fishes, Baskett; Neighbors with Wings and Fins, Johonnot.

TROUT

"It is well for anglers not to make trout, of all fishes, the prime objective of a day's sport, as no more uncertain game loves the sunlight. Today he is yours for the very asking, tomorrow, the most luscious lure will not tempt him. One hour he defies you, the next, gazes at you from some ensconcement of the fishes, and knows you not, as you pass him, casting, by.

I believe I accumulated some of this angling wisdom years ago, in a certain trout domain in New England, where there were streams and pools, ripples, cascades and drooping trees; where everything was fair and promising to the eyes for trout; but it required superhuman patience to lure them, and many a day I scored a blank. Yet on these very days when lures were unavailing, the creel empty save for fern leaves, I found they were not for naught; that the real fishing day was a composite of the weather, the wind, even if it was from the east, the splendid colors of forest trees, the blue tourmaline of the sky that topped the stream amid the trees, the flecks of cloud mirrored on the surface. The delight of anticipation, the casting, the play of the rod, the exercise of skill, the quick turns in the stream opening up new vistas, the little openings in the forest, through which were seen distant meadows and nodding flowers—all these went to make up the real trout fishing, the actual catch being but an incident among many delights.

Just how long one could be content with mere scenery in lieu of trout, I am not prepared to say; if pushed to the wall, I confess that when fishing I prefer trout to scenic effects. Still, it is a very impracticable and delightful sentiment with some truth to it, the moral being that the angler should be resourceful, and not be entirely cast down on the days when the wind is in the east.

I am aware that this method of angling is not in vogue with some, and would be deemed fanciful, indeed inane, by many more; yet it is based upon a true and homely philosophy, not of today, the philosophy of patience and contentment. "How poor are they that have not patience," said Othello. It is well to be content with things as we find them, and it is well to go a-fishing, not to catch fish alone, but every offering the day has to give. This should be an easy matter for the angler, as Walton tells us that Angling is somewhat like poetry; men are to be born so."

—FISH STORIES, JORDAN AND HOLDER

Brook stickleback
Eucalia inconstans

The Stickleback

THIS is certainly the most sagacious of the Lilliputian vertebrates; scarcely more than an inch in length when full-grown, it gazes at you with large, keen, shining-rimmed eyes, takes your measure and darts off with a flirt of the tail that says plainly, "Catch me if you can." The sticklebacks are delightful aquarium pets because their natural home is in still water sufficiently stagnant for algae to grow luxuriously; thus we but seldom need to change the water in the aquarium, which, however, should be well stocked with water plants and have gravel at the bottom.

When the stickleback is not resting he is always going somewhere and he knows just where he is going and what he is going to do, and earthquakes shall not deter him. He is the most dynamic creature in all creation, I think, except perhaps the dragon fly, and he is so ferocious that if he were as large as a shark he would destroy all other fishes. Place an earthworm, cut into small sections, in the aquarium and while each section is wrigglingly considering whether it may be able to grow both ends into another worm, the stickleback takes hold with a will and settles the matter in the negative. His ferocity is frightful to behold as he seizes his prey and shakes it as a terrier does a rat.

Well is this fish named stickleback, for along the ridge of its back are sharp, strong spines—five of them in our tiny, brook species. These spines may be laid back flat or they may be erected stiffly, making an

69

efficient saw which does great damage to fish many times larger than the stickleback. When we find the minnows in the aquarium losing their scales we may be sure they are being raked off by this saw-back; and if the shiner or sunfish undertakes to make a stickleback meal, there is only one way to do it, and that is to catch the quarry by the tail, since he is too alert to be caught in any other way. But swallowing a stickleback tail first is a dangerous performance, for the sharp spines rip open the throat or stomach of the captor. Dr. Jordan says that the sticklebacks of the Puget Sound region are called "salmon killers" and that they well earn the name; these fierce midgets unhesitatingly attack the salmon, biting off pieces of their fins and also destroying their spawn.

As seen from the side, the stickleback is slender and graceful, pointed like an arrow at the front end, and with the body behind the dorsal fin forming a long and slender pedicel to support the beautifully rounded tail fin. The dorsal fin is placed well back and is triangular in shape; the anal fin makes a similar triangle opposite it below and has a sharp spine at its front edge. The color of the body varies with the light; when floating among the water weed the back is greenish mottled with paler green, but when the fish is down on the gravel it is much darker. The lateral line is marked by a rather broad silver stripe.

If large eyes count for beauty, then the stickleback deserves "the apple," for its eyes are not only large but gemlike, with a broad iris of golden brown around the black pupil. I am convinced that the stickleback has a keener vision than most fish; it can move its eyes backward and forward rapidly and alertly. The mouth opens almost upward and is a wicked little mouth, both in appearance and action.

When swimming, the stickleback darts about rapidly, its dorsal and anal fins extended, its spines all abristle, its tail lashing the water with strong strokes and the pectorals flying so fast that they make a blur; the ventral fins are rarely extended, in fact they are nothing but two little spines. When the fish wishes to lift itself through the water it seems to depend entirely upon its pectoral fins and these are also used for balancing. Its favorite position is hanging motionless among the pond weeds, with the tail, the dorsal and ventral fins partially closed; it usually rests upon the pectoral fins which are braced against some stem; in one case I saw the ventrals and pectorals used together to clasp a stem and hold the fish in place. In moving backward the pectorals do the work, with a little beckoning motion of the tail occasionally. When resting upon the bottom of the aquarium, it closes its fins and makes itself quite inconspicuous. It can dig with much power accomplishing this by a comical augerlike motion; it plunges head first into the gravel and then by twisting the body and tail around and around, it soon forms a hiding place.

But it is as a house builder and father and home protector that the stickleback shines. In the early spring he builds him a nest made from the fine green algae called frog-spittle. This would seem a too delicate material for the house construction, but he is a clever builder. He fastens his filmy walls to some stems of reed or grass, using as a platform a supporting stem; the ones which I have especially studied were fastened to grass stems. The stickleback has a little cement plant of his own, supposed to be situated in the kidneys, which at this time of year secrete the glue for building purposes. The glue is waterproof. It is spun out in fine threads or in filmy masses through an opening near the anal fin. One species weights his platform with sand which he scoops up from the bottom, but I cannot detect that our brook stickleback does this. In his case, home is his sphere literally, for he builds a spherical house about the size of a glass marble, three-quarters of an inch in diameter; it is a hollow sphere and he cements the inside walls so as to hold them back and give room, and he finishes his pretty structure with a circular door at the side. When finished, the nest is like a bubble, made of threads of down and yet it holds together strongly.

In the case of the best known species, the male, as soon as he has finished his bower to his satisfaction, goes a-wooing; he selects some lady stickleback, and in his own way tells her of the beautiful nest he has made and convinces her of his ability to take care of a family. He certainly has fetching ways for he soon conducts her to his home. She enters the nest through the little circular door, lays her eggs within it, and then being a flighty creature, she sheds responsibilities and flits off care free. He follows her into the nest, scatters the fertilizing milt over the eggs and then starts off again and rolls his golden eyes on some other lady stickleback and invites her also to his home; she comes without any jealousy because she was not first choice, and she also enters the nest and lays her eggs and then swims off unconcernedly. Again he enters the nest and drops more milt upon the eggs and then fares forth again, a still energetic wooer. If there was ever a justified polygamist, he is one, since it is only the cares and responsibilities of the home that he desires. He only stops wooing when his nest holds as many eggs as he feels equal to caring for. He now stands on guard by the door, and with his winnowing pectoral fins, sets up a current of water over the eggs; he drives off all intruders with the most vicious attacks, and keeps off many an enemy simply by a display of reckless fury; thus he stands guard until the eggs hatch and the tiny little sticklebacks come out of the nest and float off, attaching themselves by their mouths to the pond weeds until they become strong enough to scurry around in the water.

Some species arrange two doors in this spherical nest so that a current of water can flow through and over the eggs. Mr. Eugene Barker, who has made a special study of the little five-spined sticklebacks of the Cayuga Basin, has failed to find more than one door to their nests. Mr. Barker made a most interesting observation on this stickleback's obsession for fatherhood. He placed in the aquarium two nests, one of which was guarded by its loyal builder, which allowed himself to be caught rather than desert his post; the little guardian soon discovered the unprotected nest and began to move the eggs from it to his own, carrying them carefully in his mouth. This addition made his own nest so full that the eggs persistently crowded out of the door, and he spent much of his time nudging them back with his snout. We saw this stickleback fill his mouth with algae from the bottom of the

Horned dace
Semotilus atromaculatus

aquarium, and holding himself steady a short distance away, apparently blow the algae at the nest from a distance of half an inch, and we wondered if this was his method of laying on his building materials before he cemented them.

The eggs of this species are white and shining like minute pearls, and seem to be fastened together in small packages with gelatinous matter. The mating habits of this species have not been thoroughly studied; therefore, here is an opportunity for investigation on the part of the boys and girls.

A sculpin
Cottus cognatus

LESSON

LEADING THOUGHT— The stickleback is the smallest of our common fish. It lives in stagnant water. The father stickleback builds his pretty nest of frog-spittle which he watches very carefully.

METHOD— To find sticklebacks go to a pond of stagnant water which does not dry up during the year. If it is partly shaded by bushes so much the better. Take a dip net and dip deeply; carefully examine all the little fish in the net by putting them in a Mason jar of water so that you can see what they are like. The stickleback is easily distinguished by the five spines along its back. If you collect these fish as early as the first of May and place several of them in the aquarium with plenty of the algae known as frog-spittle and other water plants they may perhaps build a nest for you. They may be fed upon bits of meat or liver chopped very fine or upon earthworms cut into small sections.

OBSERVATIONS—

1. How did the stickleback get its name? How many spines has it? Where are they situated? Are they always carried erect? How are these spines used as weapons? How do they act as a means of safety to the stickleback?

2. Describe or make a sketch showing the shape and position of the dorsal, the anal, the ventral and the pectoral fins. What is the shape of the tail? What is the general shape of the fish?

3. What is the color of the sticklebacks? Is the color always the same? What is the color and position of the lateral line?

4. Describe the eyes. Are they large or small? Can they be moved? Do you think they can see far?

5. Describe the mouth. Does it open upward, straight ahead or downward?

6. When the stickleback is swimming what are the positions and motions of the dorsal, anal, tail and pectoral fins? Can you see the ventral pair? Are they extended when the fish is swimming?

7. When resting among the pond weed of the aquarium what fins does the stickleback use for keeping afloat? How are the other fins held? What fins does it use to move backward? Which ones are used when it lifts itself from the bottom to the top of the aquarium? How are its fins placed when it is at rest on the bottom?

8. Drop a piece of earthworm or some liver or fresh meat cut finely into the aquarium and describe the action of the sticklebacks as they eat it. How large is a full-grown stickleback?

9. In what kind of ponds do we find sticklebacks? Do you know how the stickleback nest looks? Of what is it built? How is it supported? Is there one door or two? Does the father or mother stickleback build the nest? Are the young in the nest cared for? At what time is the nest built?

Supplementary reading —*Fish Stories*, Chap. XXXVI, Jordan and Holder.

Sunfish or punpkinseed
Lepomis gibbosus

The Sunfish

TEACHER'S STORY

THIS little disc of gay color has won many popular names. It is called pumpkin seed, tobacco box and sunfish because of its shape, and it is also called bream and pondfish. I have always wondered that it was not called chieftain also, for when it raises its dorsal fin with its saw crest of spines, it looks like the head-dress of an Indian chief; and surely no warrior ever had a greater enjoyment in a battle than does this indomitable little fish.

The sunfish lives in the eddies of our clear brooks and ponds. It is a near relative to the rock bass and also of the black bass and it has, according to its size, just as gamey qualities as the latter. I once had a sunfish on my line which made me think I had caught a bass and I do not know whether I or the mad little pumpkin seed was the most disgusted when I discovered the truth. I threw him back in the water but his fighting spirit was up, and he grabbed my hook again within five minutes, which showed that he had more courage than wisdom; it would have served him right if I had fried him in a pan, but I never could make up my mind to kill a fish for the sake of one mouthful of food.

Perhaps of all its names, "pumpkin seed" is the most graphic, for it resembles this seed in the outlines of its body when seen from the side. Looked at from above, it has the shape of a powerful craft with smooth, rounded nose and gently swelling and tapering sides; it is widest at the eyes and this is a canny arrangement, for these great eyes turn alertly in every direction; and thus placed they are able to discern the enemy or the dinner coming from any quarter.

The dorsal fin is a most militant looking organ. It consists of ten spines, the hind one closely joined to the hind dorsal fin, which is supported by the soft rays. The three front spines rise successively, one above another and all are united by the membrane, the upper edge of which is deeply toothed. The hind dorsal fin is gracefully rounded and the front and hind fin work independently of each other, the latter often winnowing the water when the former is laid flat. The tail is strong and has a notch in the end; the anal fin has three spines on its front edge and ten soft rays. Each ventral fin also has a spine at the front edge and is placed below and slightly behind the pectorals. The pectoral fins, I have often thought, were the most exquisite and gauzelike in texture of any fins I have ever seen; they are kept almost constantly in motion and move in such graceful flowing undulations that it is a joy to look at them.

The eye of the sunfish is very large and quite prominent; the large black pupil is surrounded by an iris that has shining lavender and bronze in it, but is more or less clouded above; the young ones have a pale silver iris. The eyes move in every direction and are eager and alert in their expression. The mouth is at the front of the body but it opens upward. The gill opening is prolonged backward at the upper corner, making an earlike flap; this, of course, has nothing to do with the fish's ears, but it is highly ornamental as it is greenish-black in color, bordered by iridescent, pale green, with a brilliant orange spot on its hind edge. The colors of the sunfish are too varied for description and too beautiful to reduce to mere words. There are dark, dull, greenish or purplish cross-bands worked out in patterns of scale-mosaic, and between them are bands of pale iridescent-green, set with black-edged orange spots. But just as we have described his colors our sunfish darts off and all sorts of shimmering, shining blue, green and purple tints play over his body and he settles down into another corner of the aquarium and his colors seem much paler and we have to describe him over again. The body below is brassy-yellow.

The beautiful colors which the male sunfish dons in spring, he puts at once to practical use. Professor Reighard says that when courting and trying to persuade his chosen one to

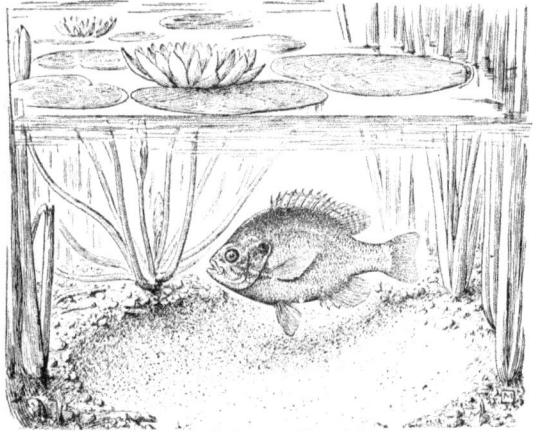
Male sunfish guarding his nest.

come to his nest and there deposit her eggs, he faces her, with his gill covers puffed out, the scarlet or orange spot on the ear-flap standing out bravely, and his black ventral fins spread wide to show off their patent-leather finish. Thus, does he display himself before her and persuade her; but he is rarely allowed to do this in peace. Other males as brilliant as he arrive on the scene and he must forsooth stop parading before his lady love in order to fight his rival, and he fights with as much display of color as he courts. But in the sunfish duel the participants do not seek to destroy each other but to mutilate spitefully each other's fins. The vanquished one with his fins all torn retires from the field. Professor Gill says: "Meanwhile the male has selected a spot in very shallow water near the shore, and generally in a mass of aquatic vegetation, not too large or close together to entirely exclude the light and heat of the sun, and mostly under an over-hanging plant. The choice is apt to be in some general strip of shallow water close by the shore which is favored by many others so that a number of similar nests may be found close together, although never encroaching on each other. Each fish slightly excavates and makes a saucer-like basin in the chosen area which is carefully cleared of all pebbles. Such are removed by violent jerks of the caudal fin or are taken up by the mouth and carried to the circular boundary of the nest. An area of fine, clean sand or gravel is generally the result, but not infrequently, according to Dr. Reighard, the nest bottom is composed of the rootlets of water plants. The nest has a diameter of about twice the length of the fish."

On the nest thus formed, the sunfish belle is invited to deposit her eggs, which as soon as laid fall to the bottom and become attached to the gravel at the bottom of the nest by the viscid substance which surrounds them. Her duty is then done and she departs, leaving the master in charge of his home and the eggs. If truth be told, he is not a strict monogamist. Professor Reighard noticed one of these males which reared in one nest two broods laid at quite different times by two females. For about a week, depending upon the temperature, the male is absorbed in his care of the eggs and defends his nest with much ferocity, but after the eggs have hatched he considers his duty done and lets his progeny take care of themselves as best they may.

Sunfish are easily taken care of in an aquarium, but each should be kept by himself as they are likely to attack any smaller fish and are most uncomfortable neighbors. I have kept one of these beautiful, shimmering pumpkin seeds for nearly a year, by feeding him every alternate day with an earthworm; these unfortunate creatures are kept stored in damp soil in an iron kettle during the winter. When I threw one of them into the aquarium he would seize it and shake it as a terrier shakes a rat; but this was perhaps to make sure of his hold. Once he attempted to take the second worm directly after the first; but it was a doubtful proceeding, and the worm reappeared as often as a prima donna, waving each time a frenzied farewell to the world.

LESSON

LEADING THOUGHT— The pumpkin seeds are very gamey little fishes which seize the hook with much fierceness. They live in the still waters of our streams or in ponds and build nests in the spring, in which the eggs are laid and which they defend valiantly.

METHOD— The common pumpkin seed in the jar aquarium is all that is necessary for this lesson. However, it will add much to the interest of the lesson if the boys who have fished for pumpkin seeds will tell of their experiences. The children should be stimulated by this lesson to a keen interest in the nesting habits of the sunfishes.

OBSERVATIONS—

1. Where are the sunfish found? How do they act when they take the hook?

2. What is the general shape of the sunfish's body as seen from above? As seen from the side? Why is it called pumpkin seed?

3. Describe the dorsal fin. How many spines has it? How many soft rays? What is the difference in appearance between the front and hind dorsal fin? Do the two act together or separately? Describe the tail fin. Describe the anal fin. Has it any spines? If so, where are they? Where are the ventral fins in relation to the pectorals? What is there peculiar about the appearance and movements of the pectoral fins?

4. Describe the eye of the sunfish. Is it large or small? Is it placed so that the fish can see on each side? Does the eye move in all directions?

5. Describe the position of the mouth. In which direction does it open?

6. What is the color of the upper portion of the gill opening or operculum? What is the general color of the sunfish? Above? Below? Along the sides? What markings do you see?

7. Where does the sunfish make its nest? Does the father or mother sunfish make the nest? Do one or both protect it? Describe the nest.

8. How many names do you know for the sunfish? Describe the actions of your sunfish in the aquarium. How does he act when eating an earthworm?

Supplementary reading —Chapters XXX, XXXVI, in *Fish Stories*, Jordan and Holder.

"The lamprey is not a fish at all, only a wicked imitation of one which can deceive nobody. But there are fishes which are unquestionably fish—fish from gills to tail, from head to fin, and of these the little sunfish may stand first. He comes up the brook in the spring, fresh as "coin just from the mint," finny arms and legs wide spread, his gills moving, his mouth opening and shutting rhythmically, his tail wide spread, and ready for any sudden motion for which his erratic little brain may give the order. The scales of the sunfish shine with all sorts of scarlet, blue, green and purple and golden colors. There is a black spot on his head which looks like an ear, and sometimes grows out in a long black flap, which makes the imitation still closer. There are many species of the sunfish, and there may be half a dozen of them in the same brook, but that makes no difference; for our purposes they are all one.

They lie poised in the water, with all fins spread, strutting like turkey-cocks, snapping at worms and little crustaceans and insects whose only business in the brook is that the fishes may eat them. When the time comes, the sunfish makes its nest in the fine gravel, building it with some care—for a fish. When the female has laid her eggs the male stands guard until the eggs are hatched. His sharp teeth and snappish ways, and the bigness of his appearance when the fins are all displayed, keep the little fishes away. Sometimes, in his zeal, he snaps at a hook baited with a worm. He then makes a fierce fight, and the boy who holds the rod is sure that he has a real fish this time. But when the sunfish is out of the water, strung on a willow rod, and dried in the sun, the boy sees that a very little fish can make a good deal of a fuss."

—David Starr Jordan.

Johnny Darter
Etheostoma nigrum

The Johnny Darter

TEACHER'S STORY

"We never tired of watching the little Johnny, or Tessellated darter (Boleo-soma nigrum), although our earliest aquarium friend (and the very first speci-mens showed us by a rapid ascent of the river weed how 'a Johnny could climb trees') he has still many resources which we have never learned. Whenever we try to catch him with the hand we begin with all the uncertainty that charac-terized our first attempts, even if we have him in a two-quart pail. We may know him by his short fins, his first dorsal having but nine spines, and by the absence of all color save a soft, yellowish brown, which is freckled with darker markings. The dark brown on the sides is arranged in seven or eight W-shaped marks, below which are a few flecks of the same color. Covering the sides of the back are the wavy markings and dark specks which have given the name the "Tessellated Darter;" but Boleosoma is a preferred name, and we even prefer 'boly' for short. In the spring the males have the head jet black; and this dark color often extends on the back part of the body, so that the fish looks as if he had been taken by the tail and dipped into a bottle of ink. But with the end of the nuptial season this color disappears and the fish regains his normal, strawy hue.*

His actions are rather bird-like; for he will strike attitudes like a tufted tit-mouse and he flies rather than swims through the water. He will, with much perseverance push his body between a plant and the sides of the aquarium and balance himself on a slender stem. Crouching catlike before a snail shell, he will snap off a horn which the unlucky owner pushes timidly out. But he is also less dainty and seizing the animal by the head, he dashes the shell against the glass or stones until he pulls the body out and breaks the shell."

—David Starr Jordan.

THE johnny darters are, with the sticklebacks, the most amusing little fish in the aquarium. They are well called darters since their movements are so rapid when they are frightened that the eye can scarcely follow them; and there is something so irresistibly comical in their bright, saucy eyes, placed almost on top of the head, that no one could help calling one of them "Johnny." A "johnny" will look at you from one side, and then as quick as a flash, will flounce around and study you with the other eye and then come toward you head-on so that he may take you in with both eyes; he seems just as interested in the Johnny out of the jar as is the latter, in the johnny within.

The johnny darter has a queer shaped body for a fish, for the head and shoulders are the larger part of him; not that he suddenly disappears into nothingness, by no means! His body is long and very slightly tapering to the tail; along his lateral line he has a row of olive-brown W's worked out in scale-mosaics; and he has some other scale-mosaics also following a pattern of angular lines and making blotches along his back. The whole upper part of his body is pale olive, which is a good imitation of the color of the brook.

The astonished and anxious look on the johnny darter's face comes from the peculiar position of the eyes which are set in the top of his forehead; they are big, alert eyes, with large black pupils, surrounded by a shining, pale yellow line at the inner edge of the green iris; and as the pupil is not set in the center of the eye, the iris above being wider than below, the result is an astonished look, as from raised eyebrows. The eyes move, often so swiftly that it gives the impression of winking. The eyes, the short snout, and the wide mouth give johnny a decidedly frog-like aspect.

Although he is no frog, yet johnny darter seems to be in a fair way to develop something to walk upon. His pectoral fins are large and strong and the ventral pair are situated very close to them; when he rests upon the gravel he supports himself upon one or both of these pairs of fins. He rests with the pectoral fins outspread, the sharp points of the rays taking hold of the gravel like toenails and thus give him the appearance of walking on his fins; if you poke him gently, you will find that he is very firmly planted on his fins so that you can turn him around as if he were on a pivot. He also uses the pectorals for swimming and jerks himself along with them in a way that makes one wonder if he could not swim well without any tail at all. The tail is large and almost straight across the end and is a most vigorous push-er. There are two dorsal fins; the front one has only nine rays; these are not branched and are therefore spines; when the fin is raised it appears almost semi-circular in shape. The hind dorsal fin is much longer and when lifted stands higher than the front one; its rays are all branched except the front one. As soon as the johnny stops swim-ming he shuts the front dorsal fin so that it can scarcely be detected; when frightened he shuts both the dorsal fins and closes the tail and the anal fin and spreads out his paired fins so that his body lies flat on the bottom; this act always reminds one of the "freezing" habit of the rabbit. But johnny does not stay scared very long; he lifts his head up inquisitively, stretching up as far as he is able on his front feet, that is, his pectorals, in such a comical way that one can hardly realize he is a fish.

The tail and the dorsal fin of the johnny darter are marked with silver dots which give them an exquisite spun-glass look; they are as transparent as gauze.

The johnny darters live in clear, swift streams where they rest on the bottom, with the head up stream. Dr. Jordan has said they can climb up water weed with their paired fins. I have never observed them doing this but I have often seen one walk around the aquarium on his fins as if they were little fan-shaped feet; and when swimming he uses his fins as a bird uses its wings. There are many species of darters, some of them the most brilliantly colored of any of our fresh-water fishes. The darters are perch-like in form.

Dr. Jordan says of the breeding habits of the darters: "On the bottom, among the stones, the female casts her spawn. Neither she nor the male pays any further attention to it, but in the breeding season the male is painted in colors as beautiful as those of the wood warblers. When you go to the brook in the spring you will find him there, and if you catch him and turn him over on his side you will see the colors that he shows to his mate, and which observation shows are most useful in frightening away his younger rivals. But do not hurt him. Put him back in the brook and let him paint its bottom with colors of a rainbow, a sunset or a garden of roses. All that can be done with blue, crimson and green pigments, in fish ornamentation, you will find in some brook in which the darters live."

LESSON

LEADING THOUGHT— The johnny darter naturally rests upon the bottom of the stream where the current is swift. It uses its two pairs of paired fins somewhat as feet in a way interesting to observe.

METHOD— Johnny darters may be caught in nets with other small fry and placed in the aquarium. Place one or two of them in individual aquaria where the pupils may observe them at their leisure. They do best in running water.

OBSERVATIONS—

1. Describe or sketch the johnny darter from above. From the side. Can you see the W-shaped marks along its side? How is it colored above?

2. How are the pectoral fins placed? Are they large or small? How are they used in swimming? Where are the ventral fins placed? How are the ventrals and dorsals used together? When resting on the bottom how are the pectoral fins used?

3. What is there peculiar about the dorsal fins of the johnny darter? When he is resting, what is the attitude of the dorsal fins? What is the difference in shape of the rays of the front and hind dorsal fins?

4. When resting on the bottom of the aquarium how is the body held? On what does it rest? In moving about the bottom slowly why does it seem to walk? How does it climb up water weed?

5. When frightened how does it act? Why is it called a darter? What is the attitude of all the fins when the fish is moving swiftly?

6. What is the shape of the tail?

7. What is there peculiar about the eyes of the johnny? Describe the eyes and their position. What reason is there in the life of the fish that makes this position of the eyes advantageous?

8. Where do we find the johnny darters? In what part of the stream do they live? Are they usually near the surface of the water or at the bottom?

"To my mind, the best of all subjects for nature-study is a brook. It affords studies of many kinds. It is near and dear to every child. It is an epitome of the nature in which we live. In miniature, it illustrates the forces which have shaped much of the earth's surface. It reflects the sky. It is kissed by the sun. It is rippled by the wind. The minnows play in the pools. The soft weeds grow in the shallows. The grass and the dandelions lie on its sunny banks. The moss and the fern are sheltered in the nooks. It comes from one knows not whence; it flows to one knows not whither. It awakens the desire to explore. It is fraught with mysteries. It typifies the flood of life. It goes on forever.

In other words, the reason why the brook is such a perfect nature-study sub-ject is the fact that it is the central theme in a scene of life. Living things appeal to children."

"Nature-study not only educates, but it educates nature-ward; and nature is ever our companion, whether we will or no. Even though we are determined to shut ourselves in an office, nature sends her messengers. The light, the dark, the moon, the cloud, the rain, the wind, the falling leaf, the fly, the bouquet, the bird, the cockroach—they are all ours.

If one is to be happy, he must be in sympathy with common things. He must live in harmony with his environment. One cannot be happy yonder nor to-morrow: he is happy here and now, or never. Our stock of knowledge of common things should be great. Few of us can travel. We must know the things at home.

Nature-love tends toward naturalness, and toward simplicity of living. It tends country-ward. One word from the fields is worth two from the city. "God made the country."

I expect, therefore, that much good will come from nature-study. It ought to revolutionize the school life, for it is capable of putting new force and enthu-

siasm into the school and the child. It is new, and therefore, is called a fad. A movement is a fad until it succeeds. We shall learn much, and shall outgrow some of our present notions, but nature-study has come to stay. It is in much the same stage of development that manual-training and kindergarten work were twenty-five years ago. We must take care that it does not crystalize into science-teaching on the one hand, nor fall into mere sentimentalism on the other.

I would again emphasize the importance of obtaining our fact before we let loose the imagination, for on this point will largely turn the results—the failure or the success of the experiment. We must not allow our fancy to run away with us. If we hitch our wagon to a star, we must ride with mind and soul and body all alert. When we ride in such a wagon, we must not forget to put in the tail-board."

—L. H. BAILEY IN THE NATURE-STUDY IDEA.

AMPHIBIANS

AMPHIBIANS

Especially during early spring, one is likely to see many frogs, toads, and salamanders about ponds and other shallow water. These animals are harmless creatures; they do not bite and their chief method of defense is to escape to some place of concealment.

While there are exceptions to the general rule, and great variations in the life habits of these animals, it may be said that they are fitted to spend certain periods of their lives on land and other periods in water. In general, the immature stages are passed in or quite near water and the young are commonly called tad poles. Of course, this means that the males and females of most species must return each year to the ponds, streams, or pools for the purpose of mating. Eggs are laid at once and usually hatch within a few days; the length of time varies according to the species and the weather conditions. To this entire group of cold blooded animals the term *amphibian* is applied; this term was selected because it really means "double life"—these animals live part of their lives on land and part in or quite near water. The presence or absence of a tail, during adult life, divides the amphibians into two more or less natural groups, the *tailed* and the *tailless amphibians*.

THE TAILLESS AMPHIBIANS

This group includes the frogs and toads. In attaining the adult stage these animals lose their tadpole tails; but we do not mean that the tail drops from the body; rather let us say that it is absorbed by the body before the animal reaches the adult stage.

Frogs and Toads

"The toad hopped by us with jolting springs."

—AKERS.

WHOEVER has not had a pet toad has missed a most entertaining experience. Toad actions are surprisingly interesting; one of my safe-guards against the blues is the memory of the thoughtful way one of my pet toads rubbed and patted its stomach with its little hands after it had swallowed a June-bug. Toads do not make warts upon attacking hands, neither do they rain down nor are they found in the bed-rock of quarries; but they do have a most interesting history of their own, which is not at all legendary, and which is very like a life with two incarnations.

TADPOLES

The mother toad lays her eggs in May and June in ponds, or in the still pools, along streams; the eggs are laid in long strings of jellylike substance, and are dropped upon the pond bottom or attached to water weeds; when first deposited, the jelly is transparent and the little black eggs can be plainly seen; but after a day or two, bits of dirt accumulate upon the jelly, obscuring the eggs. At first the eggs are spherical, like tiny black pills, but as they begin to develop, they elongate and finally the tadpoles may be seen wriggling in the jelly mass, which affords them efficient protection. After four or five days, the tadpoles usually work their way out and swim away; at this stage, the only way to detect the head, is by the direction of the tadpole's progress, since it naturally goes head first. However, the head soon becomes decidedly larger, although at first it is not provided with a mouth; it has instead, a V-shaped el-evation where the mouth should be, which forms a sucker secreting a sticky substance by means of which the tadpole attaches itself to water weeds, resting head up. When two or three days old, we can detect little tassels on either side of the throat, which are the gills by which the little creature breathes; the blood passes through these gills, and is purified by coming in contact with the air which is mixed in the water. About ten days later, these gills disappear beneath a membrane which grows down over them; but they are still used for breathing, simply having changed position from the outside to the inside of the throat. The water enters the nostrils to the mouth, passes through an opening in the throat and flows over the gills and out through a little opening at the left side of the body; this opening or breathing-pore, can be easily seen in the larger tadpoles; and when the left arm develops, it is pushed out through this convenient orifice.

The toad in various stages of development from the egg to the adult

When about ten days old, the tadpole has developed a small, round mouth which is constantly in search of something to eat, and at the same time constantly opening and shutting to take in air for the gills; the mouth is provided with horny jaws for biting off pieces of plants. As the tadpole develops, its mouth gets larger and wider and extends back beneath the eyes, with a truly toadlike expansiveness.

At first, the tadpole's eyes are even with the surface of the head and can scarcely be seen, but later they become more prominent and bulge like the eyes of the adult toad.

The tail of the tadpole is long and flat, surrounded

American toad egg mass

91

Heide Couch

Eggs of Western spadefoot. Although it looks so like our common toad, the spadefoot belongs to a different genus; it lays its eggs in cylindrical masses on submerged twigs or grass.

by a fin, thus making an organ for swimming. It strikes the water, first this side and then that, making most graceful curves, which seem to originate near the body and multiply toward the tip of the tail. This movement propels the tadpole forward, or in any direction. The tail is very thin when seen from above; and it is amusing to look at a tadpole from above, and then at the side; it is like squaring a circle.

There is a superstition that tadpoles eat their tails; and in a sense this is true, because the material that is in the tail is absorbed into the growing body; but the last thing a right-minded tadpole would do, would be to bite off its own tail. However, if some other tadpole should bite off the tail or a growing leg, these organs conveniently grow anew.

When the tadpole is a month or two old, depending upon the species, its hind legs begin to show; they first appear as mere buds which finally push out completely. The feet are long and provided with five toes, of which the fourth is the longest; the toes are webbed so that they may be used to help in swimming. Two weeks later the arms begin to appear, the left one pushing out through the breathing-pore. The "hands" have four fingers and are not webbed; they are used in the water for balancing; while the hind legs are used for pushing, as the tail becomes smaller.

As the tadpole grows older, not only does its tail become shorter but its actions change. It now comes often to the surface of the water in order to get more air for its gills, although it lacks the frog tadpole's nice adjustment of the growing lungs and the disappearing gills. At last some fine rainy day, the little creature feels that it is finally fitted to live the life of a land animal. It may not be a half inch in length, with big head, attenuated body and stumpy tail, but it swims to the shore, lifts itself on its front legs, which are scarcely larger than pins, and walks off, toeing in, with a very grown up air, and at this moment, the tadpole attains toadship. Numbers of them come out of the water together, hopping hither and thither with all of the eagerness and vim of untried youth. It is when issuing thus in hordes from the water and seen by the ignorant, that they gain the reputation of being rained down, when they really were rained up. It is quite impossible for a beginner to detect the difference between the toad and the frog tadpole; usually those of the toads are black, while those of the frogs are otherwise colored, though this is not an invariable distinction. The best way to distinguish the two is to get the eggs and develop the two families separately.

The Adult Toad

The general color of the common American toad is extremely variable. It may be yellowish-brown, with spots of lighter color, and with reddish or yellow warts. There are likely to be four irregular spots of dark color along each side of the middle of the back, and the under parts are light colored, often somewhat spotted. The throat of the male toad is black and he is not so bright in color as is the female. The warts upon the back are glands, which secrete a substance disagreeable for the animal seeking toad dinners. This is especially true of the glands in the elongated swelling or wart, above and just back of the ear, which is called the parotid gland; these give forth a milky, poisonous substance when the toad is seized by an enemy, although the snakes do not seem to mind it. Some people have an idea that the toad is slimy, but this is not true; the skin is perfectly dry. The toad feels cold to the hand because it is a cold-blooded animal, which means an animal with blood the temperature of the surrounding atmosphere; while the blood of the warm-blooded animal, has a temperature of its

A common toad, Bufo americanus.

own, which it maintains whether the surrounding air is cold or hot.

The toad's face is well worth study; its eyes are elevated and very pretty, the pupil being oval and the surrounding iris shining like gold. The toad winks in a wholesale fashion, the eyes being pulled down into the head; the eyes are provided with nictitating lids, which rise from below, and are similar to those found in birds. When a toad is sleeping, its eyes do not bulge but are drawn in, so as to lie even with the surface of the head. The two tiny nostrils are black and are easily seen; the ear is a flat, oval spot behind the eye and a little lower down; in the common species it is not quite so large as the eye; this is really the ear-drum, since there is no external ear like ours. The toad's mouth is wide and its jaws are horny; it does not need teeth since it swallows its prey whole.

The toad is a jumper, as may be seen from its long, strong hind legs, the feet of which are also long and strong and armed with five toes that are somewhat webbed. The "arms" are shorter and there are four "fingers" to each "hand;" when the toad is resting, its front

The giant toad, Bufo alvarius. The huge toad of the Southwest is from 3¼ to 6½ inches long. If molested it will secrete a fluid which is strong enough to paralyse a dog.

feet toe-in, in a comical fashion. If a toad is removed from an earth or moss garden, and put into a white wash-bowl, in a few hours it will change to a lighter hue, and vice versa. This is part of its protective color, making it inconspicuous to the eyes of its enemy. It prefers to live in cool, damp places, beneath sidewalks or piazzas, etc., and its warty upper surface resembles the surrounding earth. If it is disturbed, it will seek to escape by long leaps and acts frightened; but if very much frightened, it flattens out on the ground, and looks so nearly like a clod of earth that it may escape even the keen eyes of its pursuer. When seized by the enemy, it will sometimes "play possum," acting as if it were dead; but when actually in the mouth of the foe, it emits terrified and heart-rending cries.

The toad's tongue is attached to the lower jaw, at the front edge of the mouth; it can thus be thrust far out, and since it secretes a sticky substance over its surface, any insects which it touches adhere, and are drawn back into the mouth and swallowed. It takes a quick eye to

The little green toad. This small amphibian, resembling a lichen in appearance, is about 1½ inches long. It lives in grassy flat lands from Kansas and Colorado south into northern Mexico.

see this tongue fly out and make its catch. The tadpole feeds mostly upon vegetable matter, but the toad lives entirely upon small animals, usually insects; it is not particular as to what kind of insects; but because of the situations which it haunts, it usually feeds upon those which are injurious to grass and plants. Indeed, the toad is really the friend of the gardener and farmer, and has been most ungratefully treated by those whom it has befriended. If you doubt that a toad is an animal of judgment, watch it when it finds an earthworm and set your doubts at rest! It will walk around the squirming worm, until it can seize it by the head, apparently knowing well that the horny hooks extending backward from the segments of the worm, are likely to rasp the throat if swallowed the wrong way. If the worm prove a too large mouthful, the toad promptly uses its hands in an amusing fashion to stuff the wriggling morsel down its throat. When swallowing a large mouthful, it closes its eyes; but whether this aids the process, or is merely an expression of bliss, we have not determined. The toad never drinks by taking in water through the mouth, but absorbs it through the skin; when it wishes to drink, it stretches itself out in shallow water and thus satisfies its thirst; it will waste away and die in a short time, if kept in a dry atmosphere.

The toad burrows in the earth by a method of its own, hard to describe. It kicks backward with its strong hind legs, and in some mysterious way, the earth soon covers all excepting its head; then, if an enemy comes along, back goes the head, the earth caves in around it, and where is your toad! It remains in its burrow or hiding place usually during the day, and comes out at night to feed. This habit is an advantage, because snakes are then safely at home and, too, there are many more insects to be found at night. The sagacious toads have discovered that the vicinity of street lights is swarming with insects, and there they gather in numbers. In winter they burrow deeply in the ground and go to sleep, remaining dormant until the warmth of spring awakens them; then, they come out, and the mother toads seek their native ponds there to lay eggs for the coming generation. They are excellent swimmers; when swimming rapidly, the front legs are laid backward along the sides of the body, so as to offer no resistance to the water; but when moving slowly, the front legs are used for balancing and for keeping afloat.

The song of the toad is a pleasant, crooning sound, a sort of gutteral trill; it is made when the throat is puffed out almost globular, thus forming a vocal sac; the sound is made by the air drawn in at the nostrils and passed back and forth from the lungs to the mouth over the vocal chords, the puffed-out throat acting as a resonator.

The toad has no ribs by which to inflate the chest, and thus draw air into the lungs, as we do when we breathe; it is obliged to swallow the air instead and thus force it into the lungs. This movement is shown in the constant pulsation, in and out, of the membrane of the throat. As the toad grows, it sheds its horny skin, which it swallows; as this process is usually done strictly in private, the ordinary observer sees it but seldom. One of the toad's nice common qualities is its enjoyment in having its back scratched gently.

The toad has many enemies; chief among these is the snake and in only a lesser degree, crows and also birds of prey.

Reference— The Frog Book, Dickerson; Familiar Life in Field and Forest, Mathews; The Usefulness of the American Toad, U. S. Dept. Agr., Farmers Bulletin, No. 196.

LESSON

LEADING THOUGHT— The children should understand how to make the tadpoles comfortable and thus be able to rear them.

MATERIALS— A tin or agate pan or a deep earthenware washbowl.

THINGS TO BE DONE—

1. Go to some pond where tadpoles live.

2. Take some of the small stones on the bottom and at the sides of the pond lifting them very gently so as not to disturb what is growing on their surface. Place these stones on the bottom of the pan, building up one side higher than the other, so that the water will be more shallow on one side than on the other; a stone or two should project above the water.

3. Take some of the mud and leaves from the bottom of the pond, being careful not to disturb them and place upon the stones.

4. Take some of the plants found growing under water in the pond and plant them among the stones.

5. Carry the pan thus prepared back to the schoolhouse and place it where the sun will not shine directly upon it.

6. Bring a pail of water from the pond and pour it very gently in at one side of the pan, so as not to disarrange the plants; fill the pan nearly to the brim.

7. After the mud has settled and the water is perfectly clear, remove some of the tadpoles, which have hatched in the glass aquarium, and place in the "pond." Not more than a dozen should be put in a pan of this size, since the amount of food and microscopic plants which are on the stones in the mud, will afford food for only a few tadpoles.

8. Every week add a little more mud from the bottom of the pond or another stone covered with slime, which is probably some plant growth. More water from the pond should be added to replace that evaporated.

9. Care should be taken that the tadpole aquarium be kept where the sun will not shine directly upon it for any length of time, because if the water gets too warm the tadpoles will die.

10. Remove the "skin" from one side of a tulip leaf, so as to expose the pulp of the leaf, and give to the tadpoles every day or two. Bits of hard-boiled egg should be given now and then.

Toads' Eggs and Tadpoles

LEADING THOUGHT— The toad's eggs are laid in strings of jelly in ponds. The eggs hatch into tadpoles which are creatures of the water, breathing by gills, and swimming with a long fin. The tadpoles gradually change to toads, which are air-breathing creatures, fitted for life on dry land.

METHOD— The eggs of toads may be found in almost any pond about the first of May and may be scraped up from the bottom in a scoop-net. They should be placed in the aquarium where the children can watch the stages of development. Soon after they are hatched, a dozen or so should be selected and placed in the tadpole aquarium and the others put back into the stream. The children should observe the tadpoles every day, watching carefully all the changes of structure and habit which take place. If properly fed, the tadpoles will be ready to leave the water in July, as tiny toads.

OBSERVATIONS—

1. Where were the toads' eggs found and on what date? Were they attached to anything in the water or were they floating free? Are the eggs in long strings? Do you find any eggs laid in jellylike masses? If so, what are they? How can you tell the eggs of toads from those of frogs?

2. Is the jelly-like substance in which the eggs are placed clear or discolored? What is the shape and the size of the eggs? A little later how do they look? Do the young tadpoles move about while they are still in the jelly mass?

3. Describe how the little tadpole works its way out from the jelly covering. Can you distinguish then which is head and which is tail? How does it act at first? Where and how does it rest?

4. Can you see with the aid of a lens the little fringes on each side of the neck? What are these? Do these fringes disappear a little later? Do they disappear on both sides of the neck at once? What becomes of them? How does the tadpole breathe? Can you see the little hole on the left side, through which the water used for breathing passes?

5. How does the tail look and how is it used? How long is it in proportion to the body? Describe the act of swimming.

6. Which pair of legs appears first? How do they look? When they get a little larger are they used as a help in swimming? Describe the hind legs and feet.

7. How long after the hind legs appear before the front legs or arms appear? What happens to the breathing-pore when the left arm is pushed through?

8. After both pairs of legs are developed what happens to the tail? What becomes of it?

9. When the tadpole is very young can you see its eyes? How do they look as it grows older? Do they ever bulge out like toads' eyes?

10. As the tadpole gains its legs and loses its tail how does it change in its actions? How does it swim now? Does it come oftener to the surface? Why?

11. Describe the difference between the front and the hind legs and the front and the hind feet on the fully grown tadpole. If the tail or a leg is bitten off by some other creature will it grow again?

LESSON

LEADING THOUGHT— The toad is colored so that it resembles the soil and thus escapes the observation of its enemies. It lives in damp places and eats insects, usually hunting them at night. It has powerful hind legs and is a vigorous jumper.

METHOD— Make a moss garden in a glass aquarium jar thus: Place some stones or gravel in the bottom of the jar and cover with moss. Cover the jar with a wire screen. The moss should be deluged with water at least once a day and the jar should be placed where the direct sunlight will not reach it. In this jar, place the toad for study.

OBSERVATIONS—

1. Describe the general color of the toad above and below. How does the toad's back look? Of what use are the warts on its back?

2. Where is the toad usually found? Does it feel warm or cold to the hand? Is it slimy or dry? The toad is a cold-blooded animal, what does this mean?

3. Describe the eyes and explain how their situation is of special advantage to the toad. Do you think it can see in front and behind and above all at the same time? Does the bulge of the eyes help in this? Note

Southern toad, Bufo terrestris. The color of the Southern toads varies from red or gray to black, and in size they range in length from 1½ inches to 3½ inches. They are found from North Carolina to Florida and west to the Mississippi River

the shape and color of the pupil and iris. How does the toad wink?

4. Find and describe the nostrils. Find and describe the ear. Note the swelling above and just back of the ear. Do you know the use of this?

5. What is the shape of the toad's mouth? Has it any teeth? Is the toad's tongue attached to the front or the back part of the mouth? How is it used to catch insects?

6. Describe the "arms and hands." How many "fingers" on the "hand?" Which way do the fingers point when the toad is sitting down?

7. Describe the legs and feet. How many toes are there? What is the relative length of the toes and how are they connected? What is this web between the toes for? Why are the hind legs so much larger than the front legs?

8. Will a toad change color if placed upon different colored objects? How long does it take it to do this? Of what advantage is this to the toad?

9. Where does the toad live? When it is disturbed how does it act?

How far can it jump? If very frightened does it flatten out and lie still? Why is this?

10. At what time does the toad come out to hunt insects? How does it catch the insect? Does it swallow an earthworm head or tail first? When swallowing an earthworm or large insect, how does it use its hands? How does it act when swallowing a large mouthful?

11. How does the toad drink? Where does it remain during the day? Describe how it burrows into the earth.

12. What happens to the toad in the winter? What does it do in the spring? Is it a good swimmer? How does it use its legs in swimming?

13. How does the toad look when croaking? What sort of a noise does it make?

14. Describe the action of the toad's throat when breathing. Did you ever see a toad shed its skin?

15. What are the toad's enemies? How does it act when caught by a snake? Does it make any noise? Is it swallowed head or tail first? What means has it of escaping or defending itself from its enemies?

16. How is the toad of great use to the farmer and gardener?

References—"The Life History of the Toad," by S. H. Gage, Cornell Nature-Study Volume; The Frog Book, Dickerson.

Supplementary reading—"K'dunk, the fat one," A Little Brother to the Bear, Long.

"In the early years we are not to teach nature as science, we are not to teach it primarily for method or for drill: we are to teach it for loving—and this is nature study. On these points I make no compromise."

—L. H. Bailey.

The spring peeper, Hyla Crucifer. This small frog, measuring ¾ inch to 1½ inches in length will be found from Manitoba to Maine and southward.

The Tree-Frog, or Tree-Toad

TEACHER'S STORY

"Ere yet the earliest warbler wakes, of coming spring to tell,
From every marsh a chorus breaks, a choir invisible,
As if the blossoms underground, a breath of utterance had found."

—TABB.

ASSOCIATED with the first songs of robin and bluebird, is the equally delightful chorus of the spring peepers, yet how infrequently do most of us see a member of this invisible choir! There are some creatures which are the quintessence of the slang word "cute" which, interpreted, means the perfection of Lilliputian proportions, permeated with undaunted spirit. The chickadee is one of these, and the tree-frog is another. I confess to a thrill of delight when the Pickering's hyla lifts itself on its tiny front feet, twists its head knowingly, and turns on me the full gaze of its bronze-rimmed eyes. This is the tiniest froglet of them all, being little more than an inch long when fully grown; it wears the Greek cross in darker color upon its back, with some stripes across its long hind legs which join the pattern on the back when the frog is "shut up," as the boys say.

The reason we see so little of tree-frogs, is because they are protected from discovery by their color. They have the chameleon power of changing color to match their background. The Pickering's hyla will effect this change in twenty minutes; in this species, the darker lines forming the cross change first, giving a mottled appearance which is at once protective. I have taken three of these peepers, all of them pale yellowish brown with gray markings, and have placed one upon a fern, one on dark soil and one on the purple bud of a flower. Within half an hour, each matched its surroundings so closely, that the casual eye would not detect them. The song of the Pickering's hyla is a resonant chirp, very stirring when heard nearby; it sounds somewhat like the note of a water bird. How such a small creature can make such a loud noise, is a mystery. The process, however, may be watched at night by the light of a lamp, as none of the tree-frogs seem to pay any attention to an artificial light; the thin membrane beneath the throat swells out until it seems almost large enough to balloon the little chap off his perch. No wonder that, with such a sounding-sac, the note is stirring.

The note of the mail spring peeper is a shrill, clear call and while it is being given his throat expands into a large bubble

The green tree frog, Hyla cinerea. *These frogs, 1½ to 2½ inches long are bright green in color with a straw-colored stripe along each side. On the tips of their toes are discs which enable them to cling to vertical surfaces. The green tree frogs are found from Virginia to Texas and up the Mississippi River to Illinois*

There are several species of tree-frogs that trill in the branches above our heads all summer, and their songs are sometimes mistaken for those of the cicada, which is far more shrill.

The tree-frogs have toes and fingers ending in little round discs which secrete at will a substance by means of which they can cling to vertical surfaces, even to glass. In fact, the way to study these wonderful feet is when the frog is climbing up the sides of the glass jar. The fingers are arranged, two short inside ones, a long one, and another short one outside. The hind feet have three shorter inside toes quite far apart, a long one at the tip of the foot and a shorter one outside. When climbing a smooth surface like glass, the toes are spread wide apart, and there are other little clinging discs on their lower sides, although not so large as those at the tips. It is by means of these sticky, disc-like toes that the tree-frogs hold themselves upon the tree trunks.

The whole body of the tree-frog is covered with little tubercles, which give it a roughened appearance. The eyes are black with the iris of reddish color. The tongue is like that of other frogs, hinged to the

Common tree toad, Hyla versicolor. From Maine and southern Canada to the Gulf states is the range of these tree toads; their habitat is trees, logs, or stone fences. The color varies from ashy gray to brown or green; on the back is an irregular dark star. The eggs, in groups of thirty to forty, are attached to vegetation at the surface of the water

front of the lower jaw; it is sticky and can be thrust far out to capture insects, of which the tree-frogs eat vast numbers.

The hylas breathe by the rapid pulsation of the membrane of the throat, which makes the whole body tremble. The nostrils are two tiny holes on either side of the tip of the snout. The ears are a little below and just behind the eyes, and are in the form of a circular slit.

The eggs of the spring peepers are laid in ponds during April; each egg has a little globe of jelly about it and is fastened to a stone or a water plant. The tadpoles are small and delicate; the under side of the body is reddish and shines with metallic lustre. These tadpoles differ from those of other frogs in that they often leave the water while yet the tail is still quite long. In summer, they may be found among the leaves and moss around the banks of ponds. They are indefatigable in

Anderson tree frog, Hyla andersonii. This is a small, beautiful, green frog with a light bordered, plum-colored band along each side of its body. It lives chiefly in white cedar swamps from New Jersey to South Carolina

hunting for gnats, mosquitoes and ants; their destruction of mosquitoes, as pollywogs and as grown up frogs, renders them of great use to us. The voice of this peeper may be heard among the shrubs and vines or in trees during late summer and until November. The little creatures sleep beneath moss and leaves during the winter, waking to give us the earliest news of spring.

LESSON

LEADING THOUGHT— The prettiest part of the spring chorus of the frog ponds is sung by the tree-frogs. These little frogs have the tips of their toes specially fitted for climbing up the sides of trees.

METHOD— Make a moss garden in an aquarium jar or a two-quart can. Place stones in the bottom and moss at one side, leaving a place on the other side for a tiny pond of water. In this garden place a tree-frog and cover the jar with mosquito netting and place in the shade. The frogs may be found by searching the banks of a pond at night with a lantern. However, this lesson is usually given when by accident the tree-frog is discovered. Any species of tree-frog will do; but the Pickering's hyla, known everywhere as the spring peeper, is the most interesting species to study.

OBSERVATIONS—

1. How large is the tree-frog? What is its color? Describe the markings.

2. Place the tree-frog on some light-colored surface like a piece of white blotting paper. Note if it changes color after a half hour. Later place it upon some dark surface. Note if it changes color again. How does this power of changing color benefit the tree-frog? Place a tree-frog on a piece of bark. After a time is it noticeable?

3. Describe the eyes. Note how little the tree-frog turns its head to see anything behind it. Describe its actions if its attention is attracted to anything. What color is the pupil? The iris?

4. Note the movement of breathing. Where does this show the most? Examine the delicate membrane beneath the throat. What has this to do with the breathing?

5. What is the tree-frog's note? At what time of day does it peep? At what time of year? Describe how the frog looks when peeping.

6. How does the tree-frog climb? When it is climbing up a vertical surface study its toes. How many on the front foot? How are they arranged? How many toes on the hind foot? Sketch the front and hind feet. How do the toe-discs look when pressed against the glass? How does it manage to make the discs cling and then let go? Are there any more discs on the under side of the toes? Is there a web between the toes of the hind feet? Of the front feet?

7. Look at a tree-frog very closely and describe its nostrils and its ears.

8. Are the tree-frogs good jumpers? What is the size and length of the hind legs as compared with the body?

9. When and where are the eggs of the tree-frog laid? How do they look?

10. How do the tree-frog tadpoles differ from other tadpoles? Describe them if you have ever seen them. In what situations do they live?

11. Of what use are the tree-frogs to us?

The bullfrog, Rana catesbeiana. This is our largest frog, sometimes attaining a length of 8 inches. It is widely distributed east of the Rocky Mountains from Canada to Mexico. The bullfrog has a greenish drab back and a yellowish underside. The eggs are laid in a film, perhaps 2 feet square on the surface of still water. Its sonorous bass notes, jug-o'-rum, are heard in the evenings of early summer

The Frog

TEACHER'S STORY

THE stroller along brooksides, is likely to be surprised some day, at seeing a bit of moss and earth suddenly make a high leap and a far one, without apparent provocation. An investigation resolves the clump of moss into a brilliantly green and yellow, striped frog, and then the stroller wonders how he could have overlooked such an obvious creature. But the leopard frog is only obvious when it is out of its environment. The common green frog is quite as well protected since its color is exactly that of green pools. Most frogs spend their lives in or about water, and if caught on land, they make great leaps to reach their native element; the leopard frog and a few other species sometimes wander far afield.

Male green frog, Rana clamitans. These in habitants of deep and shallow ponds are found in eastern North America from Hudson Bay to the Gulf. In the North they are among the largest frogs, ranging from 2 to 4 inches in length. The female is shown in the following picture

Female green frog, Rana clamitans. The color of these frogs in general is greenish brown with a bright green mark from the eardrum forward along the jaw. Note that the eardrum of the male is larger than that of the female

110

In form, the frog is more slim than the toad, and is not covered with great warts; it is cold and slippery to the touch. The frog's only chance of escaping its enemies, is through the slipperiness of its body and by making long, rapid leaps. As a jumper, the frog is much more powerful than the toad because its hind legs are so much larger and more muscular, in comparison with its size. The first toe in the front feet of the leopard frog is much swollen, making a fat thumb; the mechanics of the hind legs make it possible for the frog to feather the webbed feet as it swims. On the bottom of the toes are hardened places at the joints, and sometimes others besides, which give the foot a strong hold when pushing for the jump. The toe tips, when they are pressed against the glass, resemble slightly the tree-toads' discs. The hind foot is very long, while on the front foot the toes radiate almost in a circle. The foot and leg are colored like the back of the body above, and on the under side resemble the under parts.

The frog is likely to be much more brightly colored than the toad, and usually has much of green and yellow in its dress. But the frog lives among green things, while it is to the toad's advantage to be the color of the soil. Frogs also have the chameleon power of changing color, to harmonize with their environment. I have seen a very green leopard frog change to a slate-gray when placed upon slate-colored rock. The change took place in the green portions. The common green frog will likewise change to slate-color, in a similar situation. A leopard frog changed quickly from dark green to pale olive, when it was placed in the water after having been on the soil.

The eyes of frogs are very prominent, and are beautiful when observed closely. The green frog has a dark bronze iris with a gleaming gold edge around the pupil, and around the outer margin. The eye of the leopard frog is darker; the iris seems to be black, with specks of ruddy gold scattered through it, and there is an outer band of red-gold around the margin. When the frog winks, the nictitating membrane rises from below and covers the whole eye; and when the frog makes a special effort of any sort, it has a comical way of drawing its eyes back into its head. When trying to hide at the bottom of the aquarium, the leopard species lets the eye-lids fall over the eyes, so that they do not shine up and attract pursuers.

Wood frog, Rana sylvatica. In spring these frogs are found about ponds and temporary pools in wooded areas; at other times they are in the woods. They even hibernate under stumps, stones, or logs in or near woods. Their color varies from tan to brown, a prominent black mask covering the sides of the head. They range from Quebec and Nova Scotia south to the Carolinas and westward to the plains

The ear is in a similar position to that of the toad, and in the bull-frog, is larger than the eye. In the green frog, it is a dull grayish disc, almost as large as the eye. In the leopard frog, it is not so large as the eye, and has a giltish spot at the center.

The nostrils are small and are closed when below the water, as may be easily seen by a lens. The mouth opens widely, the corners extending back under the eye. The jaws are horny and are armed with teeth, which are for the purpose of biting off food rather than for chewing it. When above water, the throat keeps up a rythmic motion which is the process of breathing; but when below water this motion ceases. The food of frogs is largely composed of insects, that frequent damp places or that live in the water.

The sound-sacs of the frogs, instead of being beneath the throat, as is the case with toads and tree-frogs, are at the side of the throat; and when inflated, may extend from just back of the eyes, out above the front legs. The song is characteristic, and pleasant to listen to, if not too close by. Perhaps exception should be made to the lay of the bullfrog, which like the song of some noted opera singers, is more wonderful than musical; the boom of the bullfrog makes the earth fairly quake. If we seize the frog by the hind leg, it will usually croak and thus demonstrate for us, the position of its sound-sacs.

Southern leopard frog, Rana sphenocephala. The home of this frog is in swamps, over flowed areas, or ponds in the southeastern states and northward along the coast to New Jersey. The pointed snout, glistening white underside, and ridges extending backward from each eye are characteristic

In addition to the snakes, the frogs have inveterate enemies in the herons which frequent shallow water, and eat them in great numbers. The frogs hibernate in mud and about ponds, burrowing deep enough to escape freezing. In the spring, they come up and sing their spring songs and the mother frogs lay their eggs in masses of jelly on the bottom of the pond, usually where the water is deeper than in the situations where the toads' eggs are laid. The eggs of the two can always be distinguished, since the toads' are laid in strings of jelly, while the frogs' are laid in masses.

It is amusing to watch with a lens, the frog tadpoles seeking for their microscopic food along the glass of the aquarium. There are horny upper and lower jaws, the latter being below and back of the former. The upper jaw moves back and forth slightly and rythmically, but the dropping of the lower jaw opens the mouth. There are three rows of tiny black teeth below the mouth and one row above; at the sides and below these teeth are little, finger-like fringes. Fringes, rows of teeth and jaws all work together, up and down, out and in, in the process of breathing. The nostrils, although minute, are present in the tadpole in its early stages. The pupil of the eye is almost circular and

Eggs of leopard frog, Rana pipiens. The eggs of the leopard frog are laid in a flattened sphere in waters of swampy marshes, overflows, and ponds. In summer, the adults are found in swampy areas, grassy woodlands, or even hay or grain fields. They range from the Pacific coast states into Mexico. The eggs of the wood frog are laid in round masses

the iris is usually yellow or copper-bronze, with black mottling. The eyes do not wink nor withdraw. The breathing-pore on the left side, is a hole in a slight protuberance.

At first, the tadpoles of the frogs and toads are very much alike; but later, most of the frog tadpoles are lighter in color, usually being olive-green, mottled with specks of black and white. The frog tadpoles usually remain much longer than the toads in the tadpole stage, and when finally they change to adults, they are far larger in size than the toads are, when they attain their jumping legs.

LESSON

LEADING THOUGHT— The frog lives near or in ponds or streams. It is a powerful jumper and has a slippery body. Its eggs are laid in masses of jelly at the bottom of ponds.

METHOD— The frog may be studied in its native situation by the pupils or it may be brought to the school and placed in an aquarium; however, to make a frog aquarium there needs to be a stick or stone projecting above the water, for the frog likes to spend part of the time entirely out of water or only partially submerged.

OBSERVATIONS—

1. Where is the frog found? Does it live all its life in the water? When found on land how and where does it seek to escape?

2. Compare the form of the frog with that of the toad. Describe the skin, its color and texture. Compare the skin of the two.

3. Describe the colors and markings of the frog on the upper and on the under side. How do these protect it from observation from above? From below? How do we usually discover that we are in the vicinity of a frog?

4. Describe the frog's ears, eyes, nostrils and mouth.

5. Compare its "hands and feet" with those of the toad. Why the difference in the hind legs and feet?

6. How does the frog feel to your hand? Is it easy to hold him? How does this slipperiness of the frog benefit it?

7. On what does the frog feed? What feeds on it? How does it escape its enemies?

8. What sounds does the frog make? Where are its sound sacs located? How do they look when they are inflated?

9. Is the frog a good swimmer? Is it a better jumper than the toad? Why?

10. Where are the frog's eggs laid? How do they look?

11. Can you tell the frog tadpoles from those of the toad? Which remains longer in the tadpole stage? Study the frog tadpoles, following the questions given on page 98.

12. What happens to the frog in winter?

This common frog Rana temporarialarva *is almost completely metamorphosed. The shape of the jaw is a bit odd still, as it has changed overnight from the algae-scraping shape to the big frog's mouth. Notice the big eyes and strong legs at this stage, and the remnants of the gill covering that also covered the front legs*

FESTINA LENTE

Once on a time there was a pool
Fringed all about with flag-leaves cool
And spotted with cow-lilies garish,
Of frogs and pouts the ancient parish.
Alders the creaking redwings sink on,
Tussocks that house blithe Bob o' Lincoln,
Hedged round the unassailed seclusion,
Where muskrats piled their cells
Carthusian;
And many a moss-embroidered log,
The watering-place of summer frog,
Slept and decayed with patient skill,
As watering-places sometimes will.
Now in this Abbey of Theleme,
Which realized the fairest dream
That ever dozing bull-frog had,
Sunned, on a half-sunk lily pad,
There rose a party with a mission
To mend the polliwog's condition,
Who notified the selectmen
To call a meeting there and then.
"Some kind of steps," they said, "are needed;
They don't come on so fast as we did:
Let's dock their tails; if that don't make 'em
Frogs by brevet, the Old One take 'em!

116

That boy, that came the other day
To dig some flag-root down this way,
His jack-knife left, and 'tis a sign
That Heaven approves of our design:
'T were wicked not to urge the step on,
When Providence has sent the weapon."
Old croakers, deacons of the mire,
That led the deep batrachian choir,
"Uk! Uk! Caronk!" with bass that might
Have left Lablache's out of sight,
Shook nobby heads, and said "No, go!
You'd better let 'em try to grow:
Old Doctor Time is slow, but still
He does know how to make a pill."
But vain was all their hoarsest bass,
Their old experience out of place,
And spite of croaking and entreating
The vote was carried in marsh-meeting.
"Lord knows," protest the polliwogs,
"We're anxious to be grown-up frogs;
But don't push in to do the work
Of Nature till she prove a shirk;
'Tis not by jumps that she advances,
But wins her way by circumstances;
Pray, wait awhile, until you know
We're so contrived as not to grow;
Let Nature take her own direction,
And she'll absorb our imperfection;
You mightn't like 'em to appear with,
But we must have the things to steer with."
"No," piped the party of reform,

"All great results are ta'en by storm;
Fate holds her best gifts till we show
We've strength to make her let them go;
The Providence that works in history,
And seems to some folks such a mystery,
Does not creep slowly on, incog.,
But moves by jumps, a mighty frog;
No more reject the Age's chrism,
Your queues are an anachronism;
No more the future's promise mock,
But lay your tails upon the block,
Thankful that we the means have voted
To have you thus to frogs promoted."
The thing was done, the tails were cropped,
And home each philotadpole hopped,
In faith rewarded to exult,
And wait the beautiful result.
Too soon it came; our pool, so long
The theme of patriot bull-frog's song,
Next day was reeking, fit to smother,
With heads and tails that missed each
other,—
Here snoutless tails, there tailless snouts;
The only gainers were the pouts.

MORAL

From lower to the higher next,
Not to the top is Nature's text;
And embryo Good, to reach full stature,
Absorbs the Evil in its nature.
—LOWELL.

THE TAILED AMPHIBIANS

The best-known representatives of this group are the salamanders of various types. Barring accidents, a salamander retains its tail throughout life. Salamanders resemble lizards in shape, and many people have incorrectly called them lizards. It is not difficult to distinguish them, if one bears in mind that the covering of the salamander is rather soft and somewhat moist, while that of the a lizard is rather dry and in the form of scales.

The red-backed salamander lacks the amphibian habits usual to the group: it lives on land during its entire life. The eggs are laid in a small cluster, in a decaying log or stump; the adult is often to be found quite near the egg cluster. On the other extreme, the mud puppies and hell benders spend their entire lives in the water. They are rarely seen, live chiefly under rocks in stream beds, and feed chiefly at night.

The many local forms of amphibians offer excellent opportunities for interesting outdoor studies.

A spotted salamander in natural surroundings

The Newt, Eft, or Salamander

Teacher's Story

AFTER a rain in spring or summer, we see these little orange-red creatures sprawling along roads or woodland paths, and since they are rarely seen except after rain, the wise people of old, declared they rained down, which was an easy way for explaining their presence. But the newts do not rain down, they rain up instead, since if they have journeys to make they must needs go forth when the ground is wet, otherwise they would dry up and die. Thus, the newts make a practice of never going out except when it rains. A closer view of the eft shows plenty of peculiarities in its appearance to interest us. Its colors are decidedly gay, the body color being orange, ornamented with vermilion dots along each side of the back, each red dot margined with tiny black specks; but the eft is careless about these decorations and may have more spots on one side than on the other. Besides these vermilion dots, it is also adorned with black specks here and there, and especially along its sides looks as if it had been peppered. The newt's greatest beauty lies in its eyes; these are black, with elongated pupils,

The red-spotted newt

almost parallel with the length of the head, and bordered above and below with bands of golden, shining iris which give the eyes a fascinating brilliancy. The nostrils are mere pinholes in the end of the snout.

The legs and feet look queerly inadequate for such a long body, since they are short and far apart. There are four toes on the front feet and five on the hind feet, the latter being decidedly pudgy. The legs are thinner where they join the body and wider toward the feet. The eft can move very rapidly with its scant equipment of legs. It has a misleading way of remaining motionless for a long time and then darting forward like a flash, its long body falling into graceful curves as it moves. But it can go very slowly when exploring; it then places its little hands cautiously and lifts its head as high as its short arms will allow, in order to take observations. Although it can see quite well, yet on an unusual surface, like glass, it seems to feel the way by touching its lower lip to the surface as if to test it. The tail is flattened at the sides and is used to twine around objects in time of need; and I am sure it is also used to push the eft while crawling, for it curves this way and that vigorously, as the feet progress, and obviously pushes against the ground. Then, too, the tail is an aid when, by some chance, the eft is turned over on its back, for with its help, it can right itself speedily. The eft's method of walking is interesting; it moves forward one front foot and then the hind foot on the other side; after a stop for rest, it begins just where

The California newt. The bright belly signals a bad meal. This salamander is quite poisonous to the touch, with skin that secretes the lethal neurotoxin tetrodotoxin.

it left off when it again starts on. Its beautiful eyes seem to serve the newt well indeed, for I find that, when it sees my face approaching the moss jar, it climbs promptly over to the other side. There are no eyelids for the golden eyes, but the eft can pull them back into its head and close the slit after them, thus making them very safe.

The eft with whose acquaintance I was most favored, was not yet mature and was afraid of earthworms; but he was very fond of plant-lice and it was fun to see the little creature stalking them. A big rose plant-louse would be squirming with satisfaction as it sucked the juice of the leaf, when the eft would catch sight of it and become greatly excited, evidently holding his breath since the pulsating throat would become rigid. There was a particularly alert attitude of the whole front part of the body and especially of the eyes and the head; then the neck would stretch out long and thin, the orange snout approach stealthily within half an inch of the smug aphid, and then there was a flash as of lightning, something too swift to see coming out of the eft's mouth and swooping up the unsuspecting louse. Then there would be a gulp or two and all would be over. If the aphid happened to be a big one, the

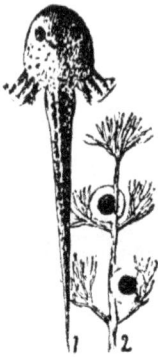

Early stage of vermilion-spotted newt.
Eggs of newt attached to water plant

eft made visible effort to swallow it. Sometimes his eftship would become greatly excited when he first saw the plant-louse, and he would sneeze and snort in a very comical way, like a dog, when eager for game.

The following is the history of this species as summarized from Mrs. S. H. Gage's charming "Story of Little Red Spot." The egg was laid in some fresh water pond or the still borders of some stream where there is a growth of water weed. The egg, which is about the size of a small pea, is fastened to a water plant. It is covered with a tough but translucent envelope, and has at the center a little yellowish globule. In a little less than a month the eft hatches, but it looks very different from the form with which we are most familiar. It has gray stripes upon its sides and three tiny bunches of red gills on each side, just back of its broad head. The tail is long and very thin, surrounded by a fin; it is an expert swimmer and breathes water as does a fish. After a time, it becomes greenish above and buff below, and by the middle of August it develops legs and has changed its form so that it is able to live upon land; it no longer has gills or fin; soon the coat changes to the bright orange hue which makes the little creature so conspicuous.

The newt usually keeps hidden among moss, or under leaves, or in decaying wood, or other damp and shady places; but after a rain, when the whole world is damp, it feels confidence enough to go out in the open, and hunt for food. For two and a half years it lives upon land and then returns to the water. When this impulse comes upon it, it may be far from any stream; but it seems to know instinctively where to go. Soon after it enters the water, it is again transformed in color, becoming olive-green above and buff below, although it still retains the red spots along the back, as mementos of its land life; and it also retains its pepper-like dots. Its tail develops a fin which extends along its back and is somewhat ruffled. In some mysterious way it develops the power to again breathe the air which is mixed with water.

122

The male has the hind legs very large and flat; the female is lighter in color and has more delicate and smaller legs. It is here in the water that the efts find their mates and finish careers which must have surely been hazardous. During its long and varied life, the eft often sheds its skin like the snake; it has a strange habit of swallowing its cast-off coat.

JACOPO WERTHER (CC BY-SA 2.0)
California Newt Egg Mass

LESSON

LEADING THOUGHT— The newts change their form three times to fit different modes of life. They are born in the water and at first have fins and gills like fishes. They then live on land, and have lungs for breathing air and lose their fins; later they go back to the water and again develop the power of breathing the oxygen contained in water, and also a fin.

METHOD—The little, orange eft or red-spotted salamander may be kept in an aquarium which has in it an object, as a stone or a clump of moss which projects above the water. For food it should be given small earthworms or leaves covered with plant lice. In this way it may be studied at leisure.

OBSERVATIONS—

1. Look at the eft closely. Is it all the same color? How many spots upon its back and what colors are they? Are there the same number of spots on both sides? Are there any spots or dots besides these larger ones? How does the eft resemble a toad?

2. Is the head the widest part of the body? Describe the eyes, the

shape and color of the pupil and of the iris. How does the eft wink? Do you think it can see well?

3. Can you see the nostrils? How does the throat move and why?

4. Are both pairs of legs the same size? How many toes on the front feet? How many toes on the hind feet? Does the eft toe-in with its front feet like a toad?

5. Does it move more than one foot at a time when walking? Does it use the feet on the same side in two consecutive steps? After putting forward the right front foot what foot follows next? Can it move backward?

6. Is the tail as long as the head and body together? Is the tail round or flat at the sides? How is it used to help the eft when traveling? Does the tail drag or is it lifted, or does it push by squirming?

7. How does the eft act when startled? Does it examine its surroundings? Do you think it can see and is afraid of you?

8. Why do we find these creatures only during wet weather? Why do people think they rain down?

9. What does the eft eat? How does it catch its prey? Does it shed its skin? How many kinds of efts have you seen?

10. From what kind of egg does the eft hatch? When is this egg laid? How does it look? On what is it fastened?

11. How many times during its life does the orange eft change color? What part of its life is spent upon land? What changes take place in its form when it leaves the water for life upon land, and what changes take place in its structure when it returns to the water?

REPTILES

REPTILES

Yet when a child and barefoot; I more than once, at morn,
Have passed, I thought, a whiplash unbraided in the sun,
When, stooping to secure it, it wrinkled, and was gone.
—EMILY DICKINSON.

THE ANIMALS in the reptile group have a covering of bony plates or scales. These animals vary greatly in size and shape an include such forms as snakes, lizards, turtles, crocodiles, and alligators. They make their homes in a great variety of places; the alligators, the crocodiles, and some of the snakes and turtles live in or near water, while many of the snakes and lizards are quite at home in desert regions.

If the teacher could bring herself to take as much interest as did Mother Eve in that "subtile animal," as the Bible calls the serpent, she might, through such interest, enter the paradise of the boyish heart instead of losing a paradise of her own. How many teachers, who have an aversion for snakes, are obliged to teach small boys whose pet diversion is capturing these living ribbons and bringing them into the schoolroom stowed away not too securely in pockets! In one of the suburban Brooklyn schools, boys of this ilk sought to frighten their teacher with their weird prisoners. But she was equal to the occasion, and surprised them by declaring that there were many interesting things to be studied about snakes, and forthwith sent to the library for books which discussed these reptiles; and this was the beginning of a nature-study club of rare efficiency and enterprise.

There are abroad in the land, many errors concerning snakes. Most people believe that they are all venomous, which is far from true. The rattlesnake still holds its own in rocky, mountainous places and the moccasin haunts the bayous of the southern coast; however, in most localities, snakes are not only harmless but are beneficial to the farmer. The superstition that if a snake is killed, its tail will live until sun-down, is general and has but slender foundation in the fact that snakes, being lower in their nerve-organization than mammals, the process of death is a slow one. Some people firmly believe that snakes spring or jump from the ground to seize their prey, which is quite false since no snake jumps clear of the ground as it strikes, nor does it spring from a perfect coil. Nor are snakes slimy, quite to the contrary,

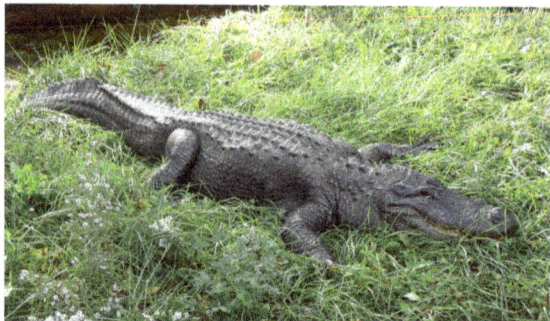

Alligator, Alligator mississippiensis. Alligators may reach a length of twelve feet; they live in or about rivers and swamps of tropical and sub-tropical regions. Their food consists chiefly of fish, mammals, and waterfowl. They are unique among reptiles in being able to produce a loud bellowing noise. In the past, alligators have been ruthlessly slaughtered and even now need more protection

they are covered with perfectly dry scales. But the most general superstition of all is that, when a snake thrusts out its tongue, it is an act of animosity; the fact is, the tongue is a sense organ and is used as an insect uses its feelers or antennae, and the act is also supposed to aid the creature in hearing; thus when a snake thrusts out its tongue, it is simply trying to find out about its surroundings and what is going on.

Snakes are the only creatures able to swallow objects larger than themselves. This is rendered possible by the elasticity of the body walls, and the fact that snakes have an extra bone hinging the upper to the lower jaw, allowing them to spread widely; the lower jaw also separates at the middle of its front edge and spreads apart sidewise. In order to force a creature into a "bag" so manifestly too small, a special mechanism is needed; the teeth supply this by pointing backward, and thus assist in the swallowing. The snake moves by literally walking on the ends of its ribs, which are connected with the crosswise plates on its lower side; each of these crosswise plates has the hind edge projecting down so that it can hold to an object. Thus, the graceful, noiseless progress of the snake, is brought about by many of these crosswise plates worked by the movement of the ribs.

Some species of snakes

Alligator eggs. More than 30 eggs may be laid by one female alligator; they are placed above water level in a nest of swamp vegetation. When hatching, the young alligators are about 8 inches long. Turtle eggs are often laid in the same pile of vegetation

simply chase their prey, striking at it and catching it in the open mouth, while others, like the black snake, wind themselves about their victims crushing them to death. Snakes can live a long time without food; many instances on record show that they have been able to exist a year or more without anything to eat. In our northern climate they hibernate in winter, going to sleep as soon as the weather becomes cold and not waking up until spring. As snakes grow, they shed their skins; this occurs only two or three times a year. The crested fly-catcher adorns its nest with these phantom snakes.

References— *The Reptile Book*, by Ditmars, gives interesting accounts of our common snakes; Mathew's Familiar *Life of Field and Forest* is also valuable. To add interest to the snake lessons let the children read "Kaa's Hunting" and "Rikki Tikki Tavi" from Kipling's *Jungle Books*.

Garter snakes

The Garter, or Garden, Snake

TEACHER'S STORY

A chipmunk, or a sudden-whirring quail,
Is startled by my step as on I fare.
A gartersnake across the dusty
Glances and—is not there.

—RILEY.

Garter snakes can be easily tamed, and are ready to meet friendly advances half way. A handsome yellow-striped, black garter lived for four years beneath our porch and was very friendly and unafraid of the family. The children of the campus made it frequent visits, and never seemed to be weary of watching it; but the birds objected to it very much, although it never attempted to reach their nests in the vine above. The garter snakes are the most common of all, in our northeastern states. They vary much in color; the ground color may be olive, brown, or black, and down the center of the back is usually a yellow, green, or whitish stripe, usually bordered by a darker band of ground-color. On each side is a similar stripe, but not so brightly colored; sometimes the middle stripe and sometimes the side stripes are broken into spots or absent; the lower side is greenish white or yellow. When fully grown this snake is two to two and one-half feet in length.

The garters are likely to congregate in numbers in places favorable for hiberna-

Common garter snake
Thamnophis sirtalis sirtalis

tion, like rocky ledges or stony sidehills. Here each snake finds a safe crevice, or makes a burrow which sometimes extends a yard or more underground. During the warm days of Indian summer, these winter hermits crawl out in the middle of the day and sun themselves, retiring again to their hermitages when the air grows chilly toward night; and when the cold weather arrives, they go to sleep and do not awaken until the first warm days of spring; then, if the sun shines hot, they crawl out and bask in its welcome rays.

After the warm weather comes, the snakes scatter to other localities more favorable for finding food, and thus these hibernating places are deserted during the summer. The banks of streams and the edges of woods are places which furnish snakes their food, which consists of earthworms, insects, toads, salamanders, frogs, etc. The young are born from late July to mid September and are about six inches long at birth; one mother may have in her brood from eleven to fifty snakelings; she often stays with them only a few hours. There are many stories about the way the young ones run down the mother's throat in case of attack; but as yet no scientist has seen this act or placed it on record. The little snakes shift for their own food, catching small toads, earthworms, and insects. If it finds food in plenty, the garter snake will mature in one year. Hawks, crows, skunks, weasels, and other predacious animals seem to find the garter snake attractive food.
SUGGESTED READING — *Holiday Hill*, by Edith M. Patch.

LESSON

THE GARTER OR GARDEN SNAKE

LEADING THOUGHT — The garter snake is a common and harmless little creature and has many interesting habits which are worth studying.

METHOD — A garter snake may be captured and placed in a box with a glass cover and thus studied in detail in the schoolroom, but the lesson should begin with observations made by the children on the snakes in their native haunts.

OBSERVATIONS —

1. What are the colors and markings of your garter snake? Do the stripes extend along the head as well as the body? How long is it?

2. Describe its eyes, its ears, its nostrils, and its mouth.

3. If you disturb it how does it act? Why does it thrust its tongue out? What shape is its tongue?

4. In what position is the snake when it rests? Can you see how it moves? Look upon the lower side. Can you see the little plates extending crosswise? Do you think it moves by moving these plates? Let it crawl across your hand, and see if you can tell how it moves.

5. What does the garter snake eat? Did you ever see one swallow a toad? A frog? Did it take it head first or tail first?

6. Where does the garter spend the winter? How early does it appear in the spring?

7. At what time of year do you see the young snakes? Do the young ones run down the throat of the mother for safety when attacked? Does the mother snake defend her young?

8. What enemies has the garter snake?

No life in earth, or air, or sky;
The sunbeams, broken silently,
On the bared rocks around me lie,—

Cold rocks with half-warmed lichens scarred
And scales of moss; and scarce a yard
Away, one long strip, yellow-barred.

Lost in a cleft! 'T is but a stride
To reach it, thrust its roots aside,
And lift it on thy stick astride!

Yet stay! That moment is thy grace!
For round thee, thrilling air and space,
A chattering terror fills the place!

A sound as of dry bones that stir
In the Dead Valley! By yon fir
The locust stops its noonday whir!

The wild bird hears; smote with the sound,
As if by bullet brought to ground,
On broken wing, dips, wheeling round!

The hare, transfixed, with trembling lip,
Halts, breathless, on pulsating hip,
And palsied tread, and heels that slip.

Enough, old friend!-'t is thou. Forget
My heedless foot, nor longer fret
The peace with thy grim castanet!

From "CROTALUS (THE RATTLESNAKE)"

—BRET HARTE

Milk snake
Lampropeltis triangulum triangulum

The Milk Snake, or Spotted Adder

TEACHER'S STORY

The grass divides as with a comb, a spotted shaft is seen,
And then it closes at your feet, and opens farther on.

—EMILY DICKINSON.

THIS is the snake which is said to milk cows, a most absurd belief; it would not milk a cow if it could, and it could not if it would. It has never yet been induced to drink milk when in captivity; and if it were very thirsty, it could not drink more than two teaspoonfuls of milk at most; thus in any case, its depredations upon the milk supply need not be feared. Its object, in frequenting milk houses and stables, is far

134

other than the milking of cows, for it is an inveterate hunter of rats and mice and is thus of great benefit to the farmer. It is a constrictor, and squeezes its prey to death in its coils.

The ground color of the milk snake is pale gray, but it is covered with so many brown or dark gray saddle-shaped blotches, that they seem rather to form the ground-color; the lower side is white, marked with square black spots and blotches. The snake attains a length of about three feet when fully grown. Although it is called commonly the spotted adder, it does not belong to the adders at all, but to the family of the king snakes.

During July and August, the mother snake lays from seven to twenty eggs; they are deposited in loose soil, in moist rubbish, in compost heaps, etc. The egg is a symmetrical oval in shape and is about one and one-eighth inches long by a half inch in diameter. The shell is soft and white, like kid leather, and the egg resembles a puffball. The young hatch nearly two months after the eggs are laid, meanwhile the eggs have increased in size so that the snakelings are nearly eight inches long when they hatch. The saddle-shaped blotches on the young have much red in them. The milk snake is not venomous; it will sometimes, in defence, try to chew the hand of the captor, but the wounds it can inflict are very slight and heal quickly.

LESSON

LEADING THOUGHT— The milk snake is found around stables where it hunts for rats and mice but never milks the cows.

METHOD—Although the snake acts fiercely, it is perfectly harmless and may be captured in the hands and placed in a glass-covered box for a study in the schoolroom.

OBSERVATIONS—

1. Where is the milk snake found? Why is it called milk snake? Look at its mouth and see if you think it could possibly suck a cow. See if you can get the snake to drink milk.

2. What does it live upon? How does it kill its prey? Can the milk snake climb a tree?

3. Where does the mother snake lay her eggs? How do the eggs

look? How large are they? How long are the little snakes when they hatch from the egg? Are they the same color as the old ones?

4. Describe carefully the colors and markings of the milk snake and explain how its colors protect it from observation. What are its colors on the under side?

5. Have you ever seen a snake shed its skin? Describe how it was done. How does the sloughed-off skin look? What bird always puts snake skins around its nest?

I have the same objection to killing a snake that I have to the killing of any other animal, yet the most humane man I know never omits to kill one.

Aug. 5, 1853.

The mower on the river meadows, when he comes to open his hay these days, encounters some overgrown water adder, full of young (?) and bold in defense of its progeny, and tells a tale when he comes home at night which causes a shudder to run through the village—how it came at him and he ran, and it pursued and overtook him, and he transfixed it with a pitchfork and laid it on a cock of hay, but it revived and came at him again. This is the story he tells in the shops at evening. The big snake is a sort of fabulous animal. It is always as big as a man's arm and of indefinite length. Nobody knows exactly how deadly is its bite but nobody is known to have been bitten and recovered. Irishmen introduced into these meadows for the first time, on seeing a snake, a creature which they have seen only in pictures before, lay down their scythes and run as if it were the Evil One himself and cannot be induced to return to their work. They sigh for Ireland, where they say there is no venomous thing that can hurt you.

—THOREAU'S JOURNAL.

Common water snake
Natrix sipedon sipedon

The Water Snake

TEACHER'S STORY

EVERY boy that goes fishing, knows the snake found commonly about mill-dams and wharves or on rocks and bushes near the water. The teacher will have accomplished a great work, if these boys are made to realize that this snake is a more interesting creature for study, than as an object to pelt with stones.

The water snake is a dingy brown in color, with crossbands of brownish or reddish brown which spread out into blotches at the side. Its color is very protective as it lies on stones or logs in its favorite attitude of sunning itself. It is very local in its habits, and generally has a favorite place for basking and returns to it year after year on sunny days.

This snake lives mostly upon frogs and salamanders and fish; however, it preys usually upon fish of small value, so it is of little economic importance. It catches its victims by chasing, and seizing them in its jaws.

It has a very keen sense of smell and probably traces its prey in this manner, something as a hound follows a fox. It is an expert swimmer, usually lifting the head a few inches above the water when swimming, although it is able to dive and remain below the water for a short time. The water snake is a bluffer, and, when cornered, it flattens itself and strikes fiercely. But its teeth contain no poison and it can inflict only slight and harmless wounds. When acting as if it would "rather fight than eat," if given a slight chance to escape, it will flee to the water like a "streak of greased lightning," as any boy will assure you.

The water snake attains a length of about four feet. The young do not hatch from eggs, but are born alive in August and September; they differ much in appearance from their parents as they are pale gray in color, with jet-black cross-bands.

LESSON

THE WATER SNAKE

LEADING THOUGHT— The water snake haunts the banks of streams because its food consists of creatures that live in and about water.

METHOD— If water snakes are found in the locality, encourage the boys to capture one without harming it, and bring it to school for observation. However, as the water snake is very local in its habits, and haunts the same place year after year, it will be better nature-study to get the children to observe it in its native surroundings.

OBSERVATIONS—

1. Where is the water snake found? How large is the largest one you ever saw?

2. Why does the water snake live near water? What is its food? How does it catch its prey?

3. Describe how the water snake swims. How far does its head project above the water when swimming? How long can it stay completely beneath the water?

4. Describe the markings and colors of the water snake. How do these colors protect it from observation? How do the young look?

5. Does each water snake have a favorite place for sunning itself?

6. Where do the water snakes spend the winter?

MAY 12, 1858.

Found a large water adder by the edge of Farmer's large mudhole, which abounds with tadpoles and frogs, on which it was probably feeding. It was sunning on the bank and would face me and dart its head toward me when I tried to drive it from the water. It is barred above, but indistinctly when out of the water, so that it appears almost uniformly dark brown, but in the water, broad, reddish brown bars are seen, very distinctly alternating with very dark-brown ones. The head was very flat and suddenly broader than the neck behind. Beneath, it was whitish and reddish flesh-color. It was about two inches in diameter at the thickest part. The inside of its mouth and throat was pink. They are the biggest and most formidable-looking snakes that we have. It was awful to see it wind along the bottom of the ditch at last, raising wreaths of mud amid the tadpoles, to which it must be a very sea-serpent. I afterward saw another, running under Sam Barrett's grist-mill, the same afternoon. He said that he saw a water-snake, which he distinguished from a black snake, in an apple tree near by, last year, with a young robin in its mouth, having taken it from the nest. There was a cleft or fork in the tree which enabled it to ascend.

—THOREAU'S JOURNAL.

The Turtle

TEACHER'S STORY

A TURTLE is at heart a misanthrope; its shell is in itself proof of its owner's distrust of this world. But we need not wonder at this misanthropy, if we think for a moment of the creatures that lived on this earth, at the time when turtles first appeared. Almost any of us would have been glad of a shell in which to retire, if we had been contemporaries of the smilodon and other monsters of earlier geologic times.

When the turtle feels safe and walks abroad for pleasure, his head projects far from the front end of his shell, and the legs, so wide, and soft that they look as if they had no bones in them, project out at the side, while the little, pointed tail brings up an undignified rear; but frighten him and at once head, legs and tail all disappear, and even if we turn him over, we see nothing but the tip of the nose, the claws of the feet and the tail turned deftly sidewise. When frightened, he hisses threateningly; the noise seems to be made while the mouth is shut, and the breath emitted through the nostrils.

The upper shell of the turtle is

Mud turtle, Kinosternon subrubrum hipocrepis, viewed from above. Many species of mud turtles are found in the eastern, central, and southern United States. The one pictured is found from Alabama to Texas and north to Kansas. When in captivity, mud turtles will eat lettuce and meat

Mud turtle viewed from below

140

called the carapace and the lower shell, the plastron. There is much difference in the different species of turtles in the shape of the upper shell and the size and shape of the lower one. In most species the carapace is sub-globular but in some it is quite flat. The upper shell is grown fast to the backbone of the animal, and the lower shell to the breast bone. The markings and colors of the shell offer excellent

Painted turtle, or terrapin, Chrysemys belli marginata. The painted turtle pictured is found from the Mississippi River eastward; but species can be found anywhere in the Unite States except in deserts and very high mountains. This turtle often swims about rocks and logs that protrude above the water

subjects for drawing. The painted terrapin has a red-mottled border to the shell, very ornamental; the wood turtle has a shell made up of plates each of which is ornamented with concentric ridges; and the box-turtle has a front and rear trap-door, hinged to the plastron, which can be pulled up against the carapace when the turtle wishes to retire, thus covering it entirely.

The turtle's head is decidedly snakelike. Its color differs with different species. The wood turtle has a triangular, horny covering on the top of the head, in which the color and beautiful pattern of the shell are repeated; the underparts are brick-red with indistinct yellowish lines under the jaw. The eyes are black with a yellowish iris, which somehow gives them a look of intelligence. The turtle has no eyelids like our own, but has a nictitating membrane which comes up from below and completely covers the eye; if we seize the turtle by the head and attempt to touch its eyes, we can see the

Chicken turtle, Deirochelys reticularia. This turtle is at home on the coastal plain from North Carolina to Mississippi. Its high shell may reach a length of eight inches; its neck is long and snakelike.

Diamond back terrapin, Malaclemys centrata. The home of the diamond back is in salt marshes from Florida to Massachusetts. In captivity it will eat lettuce, oysters, beef, chopped clams, or fish. Its flesh is used as meat and for making soup

use of this eyelid. When the turtle winks, it seems to turn the eyeball down against the lower lid.

The sense of smell in turtles is not well developed, as may be guessed by the very small nostrils, which are mere pin-holes in the snout. The mouth is a more or less hooked beak, and is armed with cutting edges instead of teeth. The constant pulsation in the throat is caused by the turtle swallowing air for breathing.

The turtle's legs, although so large and soft, have bones within them, as the skeleton shows. The claws are long and strong; there are five claws on the front and four on the hind feet. Some species have a distinct web between the toes; in others, it is less marked, depending upon whether the species lives mostly in water or out of it. The color of the turtle's body varies with the species; the body is covered with coarse, rough skin made up of various-sized plates.

The enemies of turtles are the larger fishes and other turtles. Two turtles should never be kept in the same aquarium, since they eat each others' tails and legs with great relish. They feed upon insects, small fish, or almost anything soft-bodied which they can find in the water; they are especially fond of earthworms. The species which frequent the land, feed upon tender vegetation and also eat berries. In an aquarium, a turtle should be fed earthworms, chopped fresh beef, lettuce leaves and berries. The wood turtle is especially fond of cherries.

The aquarium should always have in it a stone or some other object projecting above the water, so that the turtle may climb out, if it chooses. In winter, turtles bury themselves in the ooze at the bottom of ponds and streams. Their eggs have white leathery shells, are oblong or round, and are buried by the mother in the sand or soil near a stream or pond. The long life of turtles is a well authenticated fact, dates carved upon their shells show them to have attained the age of thirty or forty years.

The following are, perhaps, the most common species of turtles:

(a) *The Snapping Turtle*— This sometimes attains a shell 14 inches long and a weight of forty pounds. It is a vicious creature and inflicts a severe wound with its sharp, hooked beak; it should not be used for a nature-study lesson unless the specimen is very young.

(b) *The Mud Turtle*— The

MATTHEW HOOBIN (CC BY-SA 4.0)
Florida snapper, Chelydra osceola, *viewed from above. Snappers live in slow-running streams, ponds, or marshes; the female often goes some distance from her regular home to bury her round, white eggs—usually about two dozen in number.*

musk turtle and the common mud turtle both inhabit slow streams and ponds; they are truly aquatic and only come to shore to deposit their eggs. They cannot eat, unless they are under water, and they seek their food in the muddy bottoms. The musk turtle when handled, emits a very strong odor; it has on each side of the head two broad yellow stripes. The mud turtle has no odor. Its head is ornamented with greenish yellow spots.

(c) *The Painted Terrapin, or Pond Turtle*— This can be determined by the red mottled border of its shell. It makes a good pet, if kept in an aquarium by itself, but will destroy other creatures. It will eat meat or chopped fish, and is fond of earthworms and soft insects.

Spotted turtle, Clemmys guttata. *The range of the spotted turtles extends from Michigan to Maine and south to Florida. In captivity they often become very tame; they prefer raw food—earthworms, aquatic insects, ground beef, or fish.*

(d) *The Spotted Turtle*— This has the upper shell black with numerous round yellow spots upon it. It is common in ponds and marshy

A young wood turtle. Glyptemys insculpta

Box turtle, Terrapene major. *One or more species of box turtle can be found in almost any portion of the United States from the Rocky Mountains eastward.*

Soft-shelled turtle, Amyda emoryi. *The species pictured is found in Florida. Other species may be found from Canada south to the Gulf and as far west as Colorado.*

streams and its favorite perch is, with many of its companions, upon a log. It feeds under water, eating insect larvae, dead fish and vegetation. It likes fresh lettuce.

(e) *The Wood Terrapin*— This is our most common turtle; it is found in damp woods and wet places, since it lives largely upon the land. Its upper shell often reaches a length of six and one-half inches and is made up of many plates, ornamented with concentric ridges. This is the turtle upon whose shell people carve initials and dates and then set it free. All the fleshy parts of this turtle, except the top of the head and the limbs, are brick-red. It feeds on tender vegetables, berries and insects. It makes an interesting pet and will soon learn to eat from the fingers of its master.

(f) *The Box-Turtle*— This is easily distinguished from the others, because the front and rear portions of the lower shell are hinged so that they can be pulled up against the upper shell. When this turtle is attacked, it draws into the shell and closes both front and back doors, and is very safe from

144

its enemies. It lives entirely upon land and feeds upon berries, tender vegetation and insects. It lives to a great age.

(g) *The Soft-shelled Turtle*— These are found in streams and canals. The upper shell looks as if it were of one piece of soft leather, and resembles a griddle-cake. Although soft-shelled, these turtles are far from soft-tempered, and must be handled with care.

Tortoise eggs hatching.

LESSON

LEADING THOUGHT— The turtle's shell is for the purpose of protecting its owner from the attack of enemies. Some turtles live upon land and others in water.

METHOD— A turtle of any kind, in the schoolroom, is all that is needed to make this lesson interesting.

OBSERVATIONS—

1. How much can you see of the turtle when it is walking? If you disturb it what does it do? How much of it can you see then? Can you see more of it from the lower side than the upper? What is the advantage to the turtle of having such a shell?

2. Compare the upper shell with the lower as follows: How are they shaped differently? What is their difference in color? Would it be a disadvantage to the turtle if the upper shell were as light colored as the lower? Why? Make a drawing of the upper and the lower shell showing the shape of the plates of which they are composed. Where are the two grown together?

3. Is the border of the upper shell different from the central portion in color and markings? Is the edge smooth or scalloped?

4. How far does the turtle's head project from the front of the shell? What is the shape of the head? With what colors and pattern is it marked? Describe the eyes. How are they protected? How does the

A snapping turtle.

turtle wink? Can you discover the little eyelid which comes up from below to cover the eye?

5. Describe the nose and nostrils. Do you think it has a keen sense of smell?

6. Describe the mouth. Are there any teeth? With what does it bite off its food? Describe the movement of the throat. Why is this constant pulsation?

7. What is the shape of the leg? How is it marked? How many claws on the front feet? Are any of the toes webbed? On which feet are the webbed toes? Why should they be webbed? Describe the way a turtle swims. Which feet are used for oars?

8. Describe the tail. How much can be seen from above when the turtle is walking? What becomes of it, when the turtle withdraws into its shell?

9. How much of the turtle's body can you see? What is its color? Is it rough or smooth?

10. What are the turtle's enemies? How does it escape from them? What noise does the turtle make when frightened or angry?

146

11. Do all turtles live for part of the time in water? What is their food and where do they find it? Write an account of all the species of turtles that you know.

12. How do turtle eggs look? Where are they laid? How are they hidden?

SUPPLEMENTAL READING—"Turtle Eggs for Agassiz," Dallas Lore Sharp, Atlantic Monthly, Feb., 1910.

INVERTEBRATES

THE GARDEN SNAIL

PERCHANCE if those who speak so glibly of a "snail's pace" should study it, they would not sneer at it, for carefully observed, it seems the most wonderful method of locomotion ever devised by animal. Naturally enough, the snail cannot gallop since it has but one foot; but it is safe to assert that this foot, which is the entire lower side of the body, is a remarkable organ of locomotion. Let a snail crawl up the side of a tumbler and note how this foot stretches out and holds on. It has flanges along the sides, which secrete an adhesive substance that enables the snail to cling, and yet it also has the power of letting go at will. The slow, even, pushing forward of the whole body, weighted by the unbalanced shell, is as mysterious and seemingly as inevitable, as the march of fate, so little is the motion connected with any apparent muscular effort. But when his snailship wishes to let go and retire from the world, this foot performs a feat which is certainly worthy of a juggler; it folds itself lengthwise, and the end on which the head is retires first into the shell, the tail end of the foot being the last to disappear. And now find your snail!

Never was an animal so capable of stretching out and then folding up all its organs, as is this little tramp who carries his house with him. Turn one on his back when he has withdrawn into his little hermitage, and watch what happens. Soon he concludes he will find out

where he is, and why he is bottomside up; as the first evidence of this, the hind end of the foot, which was folded together, pushes forth; then the head and horns come bubbling out. The horns are not horns at all, but each

A snail searching for food

is a stalk bearing an eye on the tip. This is arranged conveniently, like a marble fastened to the tip of a glove finger. When a snail wishes to see, it stretches forth the stalk as if it were made of rubber; but if danger is perceived, the eye is pulled back exactly as if the marble were pulled back through the middle of the glove finger; or as a boy would say, "it goes into the hole and pulls the hole in after it." Just below the stalked eyes, is another pair of shorter horns, which are feelers, and which may be drawn back in the same manner; they are used constantly for testing the nature of the surface on which the snail is crawling. It is an interesting experiment to see how near to the eyes and the feelers we can place an object, before driving them back in. With these two pairs of sense organs pushed out in front of him, the snail is well equipped to observe the topography of his immediate vicinity; if he wishes to explore above, he can stand on the tip of his tail and reach far up; and if there is anything to take hold of, he can glue his toe fast to it and pull himself up. Moreover, I am convinced that snails have decided views about where they wish to go, for I have tried by the hour to keep them marching lengthwise on the piazza railing, so as to study them; and every snail was determined to go crosswise and crawl under the edge, where it was nice and dark.

It is interesting to observe through a lens, the way a snail takes his dinner; place before him a piece of sweet apple or other soft fruit, and he will lift himself on his front toe and begin to work his way into the fruit. He has an efficient set of upper teeth, which look like a saw and are colored as if he chewed tobacco; with these teeth and with his round tongue, which we can see popping out, he soon makes an ap-

Tree snails

preciable hole in the pulp; but his table manners are not nice, since he is a hopeless slobberer.

There are right and left spiraled snails. All those observed for this lesson show the spiral wound about the center from left over to right, or in the direction of the movement of the hands of a clock, and this is usually the case. With the spiral like this, the breathing pore is on the right side of the snail and may be seen as an opening where the snail joins the shell. This pore may be seen to open and contract slowly; by this motion, the air is sucked into the shell where it bathes the snail's lung, and is then forced out—a process very similar to our own breathing.

The snail has good judgment when attacked; at the first scare, he simply draws in his eyes and feelers and withdraws his head, so that nothing can be seen of him from above, except a hard shell which would not attract the passing bird. But if the attack continues, he lets go all hold on the world, and nothing can be seen of him but a little mass which blocks the door to his house; and if he is obliged to experience a drought, he makes a pane of glass out of mucus across his door, and thus stops evaporation. This is a very wise precaution, because

Slug with eye stalks extended. Slug are relatives of land snails but they have no shells

the snail is made up largely of moisture and much water is needed to keep his mucilage factory running.

The way the snail uses his eyes is comical; he goes to the edge of a leaf and pokes one eye over to see what the new territory is like; but if his eye strikes an object, he pulls that one back, and prospects for a time with the other. He can lengthen the eye-stalk amazingly if he has need. How convenient for us if we could thus see around a corner. If a small boy were as well off as a snail, he could see the entire ball game through a knot-hole in the fence. In fact, the more we study the snail, the more we admire, first his powers of ascertaining what there is in the world, and then his power of getting around in the world by climbing recklessly and relentlessly over obstacles, not caring whether he is right side up on the floor or hanging wrong side up from the ceiling; and, finally, we admire his utter reticence when things do not go to suit him. I think the reason I always call a snail "he" is because he seems such a philosopher—a Diogenes in his tub. However, since the snail combines both sexes in one individual the pronoun is surely applicable.

When observed through a lens, the snail's skin looks like that of the alligator, rough and divided into plates, with a surface like pebbled leather; and no insect intruder can crawl up his foot and get into the shell "unbeknownst," for the shell is grown fast to the flange, that grows out of the middle of the snail's back. The smoother the surface the snail is crawling upon, the harder to make him let go. The reason for this lies in the mucus, which he secretes as he goes, and which enables him to fasten himself anywhere; he can crawl up walls or beneath any horizontal surface, shell downward, and he leaves a shining trail behind him wherever he goes.

Snail eggs are as large as small peas, almost transparent, covered with very soft shells, and fastened together by mucus. They are laid under stones and decaying leaves. As soon as the baby snail hatches, it has a shell with only one spiral turn in it; as it grows, it adds layer after layer to the shell on the rim about the opening—which is called the lip; these layers we can see as ridges on the shell. If we open an empty shell, we can see the progress of growth in the size of the spirals. Snails eat succulent leaves and other soft vegetable matter. During the winter, they bury themselves beneath objects or retire into soft humus. In preparing for the winter, the snail makes a door of mucus and lime, or sometimes three doors, one behind another, across the entrance to his shell, leaving a tiny hole to admit the air. There are varieties of snails which are eaten as dainties in Europe, and are grown on snail farms for the markets. The species most commonly used is the same as that which was regarded as a table luxury by the ancient Romans.

References— Wild Life, Ingersoll; The Natural History of Some Common Animals, Latter.

LESSON

LEADING THOUGHT— The snail carries his dwelling with him, and retires within it in time of danger. He can climb on any smooth surface.

METHOD— The pupils should make a snailery, which may consist of any glass jar, with a little soil and some moss or leaves at the bottom, and a shallow dish of water at one side. The moss and soil should be kept moist. Place the snails in this and give them fresh leaves or pulpy fruit, and they will live comfortably in confinement. A bit of cheese-cloth fastened with a rubber band should be placed over the top of the jar. A tumbler inverted over a dish, on which is a leaf or two, makes a good observation cage to pass around the room for closer examination. An empty shell should be at hand, which may be opened and examined.

OBSERVATIONS—

1. Where do you find snails? Why do they like to live in such places?
2. How does a snail walk? Describe its "foot." How can it move with

only one foot? Describe how it climbs the side of the glass jar. How does it cling?

3. What sort of a track does a snail leave behind it? What is the use of this mucus?

4. Where are the snail's eyes? Why is this arrangement convenient? If we touch one of the eyes what happens? What advantage is this to the snail? Can it pull in one eye and leave the other out?

5. Look below the eyes for a pair of feelers. What happens to these if you touch them?

6. What is the use of its shell to a snail? What does the snail do if startled? If attacked? When a snail is withdrawn into its shell can you see any part of the body? Is the shell attached to the middle of the foot? How did the shell grow on the snail's back? How many spiral turns are there in the full-grown shell? Are there as many in the shell of a young snail? Can you see the little ridges on the shell? Do you think that these show the way the shell grew?

7. Can you find the opening through which the snail draws its breath? Where is this opening? Describe its action.

8. Put the snail in a dry place for two or three days, and see what happens. Do you think this is for the purpose of keeping in moisture? What does the snail do during the winter?

9. Place a snail on its back and see how it rights itself. Describe the way it eats. Can you see the horny upper jaw? Can you see the rasping tongue? What do snails live on?

10. Do you know how the snail eggs look and where they are laid? How large is the shell of the smallest garden snail you ever saw? How many spiral turns were there in it? Open an empty snail shell and see how the spirals widened as the snail grew. Do you think the shell grew by layers added to the lip?

11. Do all snails have shells? Describe all the kinds of snails you know. What people consider snails a table delicacy?

TO A SNAIL

Little Diogenes hearing your tub,
whither away so gay,
With your eyes on stalks, and a foot that walks,

tell me this I pray!
Is it an honest snail you seek
that makes you go so slow.
And over the edges of all things peek?
Have you found him, I want to know;
Or do you go slow because you knew,
your house is near and tight?
And there is no hurry and surely no worry
lest you stay out late at night.

The Earthworm

ALTHOUGH not generally considered attractive, for two reasons the earthworm has an important place in nature-study: it furnishes an interesting example of lowly organized creatures, and it is of great economic importance to the agriculturist. The lesson should have special reference to the work done by earthworms and to the simplicity of the tools with which the work is done.

The earthworm is, among lower animals, essentially the farmer. Long before man conceived the idea of tilling the soil, this seemingly insignificant creature was busily at work plowing, harrowing, and fertilizing the land. Nor did it overlook the importance of drainage and the addition of amendments—factors of comparatively recent development in the management of the soil by man.

Down into the depths, sometimes as far as seven or eight feet, but usually from twelve to eighteen inches, goes the little plowman, bringing to the surface the subsoil, which is exactly what we do when we plow deeply. To break up the soil as our harrows do, the earthworm grinds it in a gizzard stocked with grains of sand or fine gravel, which

act as millstones. Thus it turns out soil of much finer texture than we, by harrowing or raking, can produce. In its stomach it adds the lime amendment, so much used by the modern farmer. The earthworm is apparently an adept in the use of fertilizers; it even shows discrimination in keeping the organic matter near the surface, where it may be incorporated into the soil of the root zone. It drags into its burrows dead leaves, flowers and grasses, with which to line the upper part. Bones of dead animals, shells, and twigs are buried by it, and, being more or less decayed, furnish food for plants. These minute agriculturists have never studied any system of drainage, but they bore holes to some depth which carry off the surplus water. They plant seeds by covering those that lie on the ground with soil from below the surface—good, enriched, well granulated soil it is, too. They further care for the growing plants by cultivating, that is keeping fine and granular, the soil about the roots.

It was estimated by Darwin that, in garden soil in England, there are more than 50,000 earthworms in an acre, and that the whole superficial layer of vegetable mold passes through their bodies in the course of every few years, at the rate of eighteen tons per acre yearly.

This agricultural work of the earthworm has been going on for ages. Wild land owes much of its beauty to this diminutive creature which keeps the soil in good condition. The earthworm has undermined and buried rocks, changing greatly the aspect of the landscape. It has preserved ruins and ancient works of art. Several Roman villas in England owe their preservation to the earthworm. All this work is accomplished with the most primitive tools, a tiny proboscis, a distensible pharynx, a rather indeterminate tail, a gizzard and the calcareous glands peculiar to this lowly creature.

An earthworm has a peculiar, crawling movement. Unlike the snake, which also moves without legs, it has no scales to function in part as legs; but it has a very special provision for locomotion. On the under side of a worm are found numerous *setae*—tiny, bristlelike projections. These will be seen to be in double rows on each segment, excepting the first three and the last. The setae turn so that they point in the opposite direction from which the worm is moving. It is this use of these clinging bristles, together with strong muscles, which enables a worm to hold tightly to its burrow when bird or man attempts its removal. A piece of round elastic furnishes an excellent example of contraction and extension, such as the earthworm exhibits. Under the skin of the worm are two sets of muscles the outer passing in circular direction around the body, the inner running lengthwise. The movement of these maybe easily seen in a good-sized, living specimen. The body is lengthened by the contraction of circular and the extension of longitudinal muscles, and shortened by the opposite movement.

The number of segments may vary with the age of the worm. In the immature, the *clitellum,* a thick, whitish ring near the end, is absent. The laying of the earthworm's egg is an interesting performance. A saclike ring is formed about the body in the region of the clitellum. This girdle is gradually worked forward and, as it is cast over the head, the sac-ends snap together enclosing the eggs. These capsules, yellowish-brown, football-shaped, about the size of a grain of wheat, may be found in May or June about manure piles or under stones.

Earthworms are completely deaf, although sensitive to vibration. They have no eyes, but can distinguish between light and darkness. The power of smell is feeble. The sense of taste is well developed; the sense of touch is very acute; and we are not so sure as is Dr. Jordan, that the angleworm is at ease on the hook.

Any garden furnishes good examples of the home of the earthworm. The burrows are made straight down at first, then wind about irregularly. Usually they are about one or two feet deep, but may reach even eight feet. The burrow terminates generally in an enlargement where one or several worms pass the winter. Toward the surface, the burrow is lined with a thin layer of fine, dark colored earth, voided by the worm. This creature is an excavator and builder of no mean ability. The towerlike "castings" so characteristic of the earthworm, are formed with excreted earth. Using the tail as a trowel, it places earth, now on one side and now on the other. In this work, of course, the tail protrudes; in the search for food, the head is out. A worm, then, must make its home, narrow as it is, with a view to being able to turn in it.

An earthworm will bury itself in loose earth in two or three minutes, and in compact soil, in fifteen minutes. Pupils should be able to make these observations easily either in the terrarium or in the garden.

In plugging the mouths of their burrows, earthworms show something that seems like intelligence. Triangular leaves are invariably drawn in by the apex, pine-needles by the common base, the manner varying with the shape of the leaf. They do not drag in a leaf by the footstalk, unless its basal part is as narrow as the apex. The mouth of the burrow may be lined with leaves for several inches.

The burrows are not found in dry ground nor in loose sand. The earthworm lives in the finer, moderately wet soils. It must have moisture since it breathes through the skin, and it has sufficient knowledge of soil texture and plasticity to recognize the futility of attempts at burrow building with unmanageable, large grains of sand.

These creatures are nocturnal, rarely appearing by day unless "drowned out" of the burrows. During the day they lie near the surface extended at full length, the head uppermost. Here they are discovered by keen-eyed birds and sacrificed by thousands, notwithstanding the strong muscular protest of which they are capable.

Seemingly conscious of its inability to find the way back to its home, an earthworm anchors tight by its tail while stretching its elastic length in a foraging expedition. It is an omnivorous creature, including in its diet earth, leaves, flowers, raw meat, fat, and even showing cannibalistic designs on fellow earthworms. In the schoolroom, earthworms may be fed on pieces of lettuce or cabbage leaves. A feeding worm will show the proboscis, an extension of the upper lip used to push food into the mouth. The earthworm has no hard jaws or teeth, yet it eats through the hardest soil. Inside the mouth opening is a very muscular pharynx, which can be extended or withdrawn. Applied to the surface of any small object it acts as a suction pump, drawing food into the food tube. The earth taken in furnishes some organic matter for food; calcareous matter is added to the remainder before being voided. This process is unique among animals. The calcareous matter is supposed to be derived from leaves which the worms eat. Generally the earth is swallowed at some distance below the surface, and finally ejected in characteristic "castings." Thus, the soil is slowly worked over and kept in good condition by earthworms, of which Darwin says: "It may be doubted whether there are many other animals which have played so important a part in the history of the world as have these lowly organized creatures."

References— The Earthworm, Darwin; The Natural History of Some Common Animals, Latter.

"*Fly fishing is an art, a fine art beyond a doubt, but it is an art and, like all art, it is artificial. Fishing with an angleworm is natural. It fits into the need of the occasion. It fits in with the spirit of the boy. It is not by chance that the angleworm, earthworm, fishworm, is found in every damp bank, in every handy bit of sod, the green earth over, where there are races whose boys are real boys with energy enough to catch a fish. It is not by chance that the angleworm makes a perfect fit on a hook, with no anatomy with which to feel pains, and no arms or legs to be broken off or to be waved helplessly in the air. Its skin is tough enough so as not to tear, not so tough as to receive unseemly bruises, when the boy is placing it on the hook. The angleworm is perfectly at home on the hook. It is not quite comfortable anywhere else. It crawls about on sidewalks after rain, bleached and emaciated. It is never quite at ease even in the ground, but on the hook it rests peacefully, with the apparent feeling that its natural mission is performed.*"
—"Boys' Fish and Boys' Fishing," by David Starr Jordan.

LESSON

LEADING THOUGHT— The earthworm is a creature of the soil and is of much economic importance.

METHOD— Any garden furnishes abundant material for the study of earthworms. They are nocturnal workers and may be observed by lantern light. To form some estimate of the work done in a single night, remove the "casts" from a square yard of earth one day, and examine that piece of earth the next. It is well to have a terrarium in the schoolroom for frequent observation. Scatter grass or dead leaves on top of the soil, and note what happens. For the study of the individual worm and its movements, each pupil should have a worm with some earth upon his desk.

OBSERVATIONS—

1. How does the earthworm crawl? How does it turn over? Has it legs? Compare its movement with that of a snake, another legless animal. What special provision for locomotion has the earthworm?

2. Compare the lengths of the contracted and extended body. How accounted for?

3. Describe the body—its shape and color, above and below. Examine the segments. Do all the worms have the same number? Compare the head end with the tail end of the body. Has every worm a "saddle," or clitellum?

4. Does the earthworm hear easily? Has it eyes? Is it sensible to smell or to touch? What sense is most strongly developed?

5. Describe the home of the earthworm. Is it occupied by more than one worm? How long does it take a worm to make a burrow? How does it protect its home? How does it make a burrow? In what kind of soil do you find earthworms at work?

6. Is the earthworm seen most often at night or by day? Where is it the rest of the time? How does it hold to its burrow? When is the tail end at the top? When the head end?

7. What is the food of the earthworm? How does it get its food?

8. Look for the eggs of the earthworm about manure piles or under stones.

9. What are the enemies of the earthworm? Is it a friend or an enemy to us? Why?

10. The earthworm is a good agriculturist. Why?

The Crayfish

WHEN I look at a crayfish I envy it, so rich is it in organs with which to do all that it has to do. From the head to the tail, it is crowded with a large assortment of executive appendages. In this day of multiplicity of duties, if we poor human creatures only had the crayfish's capabilities, then might we hope to achieve what lies before us.

The most striking thing in the appearance of the crayfish is the great pair of nippers on each of the front legs. Wonderfully are its "thumb and finger" put together; the "thumb" is jointed so that it can move back and forth freely; and both are armed, along the inside edge, with saw teeth and with a sharp claw at the tip so that they can get a firm grip upon an object. Five segments in these great legs can be easily seen; that joining the body is small, but each successive one is wider and larger, to the great forceps at the end. The two stout segments behind the nippers give strength, and also a suppleness that enables the claws to be bent in any direction.

The legs of the pair behind the big nippers have five segments readily visible; but these legs are slender and the nippers at the end are small; the third pair of legs is armed like the second pair; but the fourth and fifth pairs lack the pincers, and end in a single claw.

But the tale of the crayfish's legs is by no means told; for between and above the great pincers is a pair of short, small legs tipped with single claws, and fringed on their inner edges. These are the maxillapeds, or jaw-feet; and behind them, but too close to be seen easily, are two more pairs of jaw-feet. As all of these jaw-feet assist at meals, the crayfish apparently always has a "three fork" dinner; and as if to provide accommodations for so many eating utensils, it has three pairs of jaws all working sidewise, one behind the other. Two of these pairs are maxillae and one, mandibles. The mandibles are the only ones we see as we look in between the jaw-feet; they are notched along the biting edge. Connected with the maxillae, on each side, are two pairs of threadlike flappers, that wave back and forth vigorously and have to do with setting up currents of water over the gills.

Thus we see that, in all, the crayfish has three pairs of jaw-feet, one pair of great nippers and four pairs of walking feet, two of which also have nippers and are used for digging and carrying.

When we look upon the crayfish from above, we see that the head and thorax are fastened solidly together, making what is called a cephalothorax. The cephalothorax is covered with a shell called the carapace, which is the name given also to the upper part of the turtle's shell. The suture where the head joins the thorax is quite evident. In

*A Snow White Crayfish (*Procambarus sp.*) and a mystery snail are fighting over for food*

looking at the head, the eyes first attract our attention; each is black and oval and placed on the tip of a stalk, so it can be extended or retracted or pushed in any direction, to look for danger. These eyes are like the compound eyes of insects, in that they are made up of many small eyes, set together in a honeycomb pattern.

The long antennae are as flexible as braided whiplashes, large at the base and ending in a threadlike tip. They are composed of many segments, the basal ones being quite large. Above the antennae on each side, is a pair of shorter ones called antennules, which come from the same basal segment; the lower one is the more slender and is usually directed forward; the upper one is stouter, curves upward, and is kept always moving, as if it were constantly on the alert for impressions. The antennae are used for exploring far ahead or behind the creature, and are often thrust down into the mud and gravel at the bottom of the aquarium, as if probing for treasure. The antennules seem to give warning of things closer at hand. Between the antennae and antennules is a pair of fingerlike organs, that are hinged at the outer ends and can be lifted back, if we do it carefully.

In looking down upon a crayfish, we can see six abdominal segments and the flaring tail at the end, which is really another segment greatly modified. The first segment, or that next to the cephalothorax, is narrow; the others are about equal in size, each graceful in shape, with a widened part at each side which extends down along the sides of the creature. These segments are well hinged together so that the abdomen may be completely curled beneath the cephalothorax. The plates along the sides are edged with fringe. The tail consists of five parts, one semicircular in the center, and two fan-shaped pieces at each side, and all are margined with fringe. This tail is a remarkable organ. It can be closed or extended sidewise like a fan; it can be lifted up or curled beneath.

Looking at the crayfish from below, we see on the abdomen some very beautiful featherlike organs called swimmerets. Each swimmeret consists of a basal segment with twin paddles joined to its tip, each paddle being narrow and long and fringed with hairs. The mother crayfish has four pairs of these, one pair on each of the second, third, fourth and fifth segments; her mate has an additional larger pair on the first segment. These swimmerets, when at rest, lie close to the abdomen and are directed forward and slightly inward. When in motion, they paddle with a backward, rhythmic motion, the first pair setting the stroke and the other pairs following in succession. This motion sends the body forward, and the swimmerets are chiefly used to aid the legs in forward locomotion. A crayfish, on the bottom of a pond, seems to glide about with great ease; but place it on land, and it is an awkward walker. The reason for this difference lies, I believe, in the aid given by the swimmerets when the creature is in water. Latter says: "In walking, the first three pairs of legs pull and the fourth pair pushes. Their order of movement is as follows: The first on the right and the third on the left side move together, next the third right and the first left, then the second right and fourth left, and lastly the fourth right and second left."

When the crayfish really wishes to swim, the tail is suddenly brought into use; it is thrust out backward, lays hold of the water by spreading out widely, and then doubles under with a spasmodic jerk which pulls the creature swiftly backward.

The crayfish's appearance is magically transformed when it begins to swim; it is no longer a creature of sprawling awkward legs and great clumsy nippers; now, its many legs lie side by side supinely and the great claws are limp and flow along in graceful lines after the body, all obedient to the force which sends the creature flying through the water. I cannot discover that the swimmerets help in this movement.

The mother crayfish has another use for her swimmerets; in the spring, when she is ready to lay eggs, she cleans off her paddles with her hind legs, covers them with waterproof glue, and then plasters her eggs on them in grapelike clusters of little dark globules. What a nice way to look after her family! The little ones hatch, but remain clinging to the maternal swimmerets, until they are large enough to scuttle around on the brook bottom and look out for themselves.

The breathing apparatus of the crayfish cannot be seen without dissection. All the walking legs, except the last pair, have gills attached to that portion of them which joins the body, and which lies hidden underneath the sides of the carapace or shell. The blood is forced into these gills, sends off its impurities through their thin walls and takes

A land crab, a relative of the crayfish. Note the eye-stalks

in the oxygen from the water, currents of which are kept steadily flowing forward.

Crayfishes haunt still pools along brooksides and river margins and the shallow ponds of our fresh waters. There they hide beneath sticks and stones, or in caves of their own making, the doors of which they guard with the big and threatening nippers, which stand ready to grapple with anybody that comes to inquire if the folks are at home. The upper surface of the crayfish's body is always so nearly the color of the brook bottom, that the eye seldom detects the creature until it moves; and if some enemy surprises one, it swims off with terrific jerks which roil all the water around and thus covers its retreat. In the winter, our brook forms hibernate in the muddy bottoms of their summer haunts. There are many species; some in our Southern States, when the dry season comes on, live in little wells which they dig deep enough to reach water. They heap up the soil which they excavate around the mouth of the well, making well-curbs of mud; these are ordinarily called "crawfish chimneys." The crayfishes find their food in the flotsam and jetsam of the pool. They seem fond of the flesh of dead fishes and are often trapped by its use as bait.

The growth of the crayfish is like that of insects; as its outer covering is a hard skeleton that will not stretch, it is shed as often as necessary; it breaks open down the middle of the back of the carapace, and the soft-bodied creature pulls itself out, even to the last one of its claws. While its new skin is yet elastic, it stretches to its utmost; but this skin also hardens after a time and is, in its turn, shed. Woe to the crayfish caught in this helpless, soft condition after molting! For

*Fiddler crabs, so called from the position in which the male often holds
the enlarged claw, are burrowing crabs of the Atlantic coast*

it then has no way to protect itself. We sometimes find the old skin floating, perfect in every detail, and so transparent that it seems the ghost of a crayfish.

Not only is the crayfish armed in the beginning with a great number of legs, antennae, etc., but if it happens to lose any of these organs, they will grow again. It is said that, when attacked, it can voluntarily throw off one or more of its legs. We have often found one of these creatures with one of the front claws much larger than the other; it had probably lost its big claw in a fight, and the new growth was not yet completed.

I have been greatly entertained by watching a female crayfish make her nest in my aquarium which has, for her comfort, a bottom of three inches of clean gravel. She always commences at one side by thrusting down her antennae and nippers between the glass and stones; she seizes a pebble in each claw and pulls it up and in this way starts her excavation; but when she gets ready to carry off her load, she comes to the task with her tail tucked under her body, as a lady tucks up her skirts when she has something to do that requires freedom of movement. Then with her great nippers and the two pairs of walking feet, also armed with nippers, she loads up as much as she can carry between her great claws and her breast. She keeps her load from overflowing by holding it down with her first pair of jaw-feet, just as I have seen a schoolboy use his chin, when carrying a too large load of books; and she keeps the load from falling out by supporting it from beneath with her first pair of walking legs. Thus, she starts off with her "apron" full, walking on three pairs of feet, until she gets to the dumping place; then she suddenly lets go and at the same time her tail straightens out with a gesture which says plainly, "There!" Sometimes when she gets a very large load, she uses her second pair of walking legs to hold up the burden, and crawls off successfully, if not with ease, on two pairs of legs,—a most unnatural quadruped.

I had two crayfishes in a cage in an aquarium, and each made a nest in the gravel at opposite ends of the cage, heaping up the debris into a partition between them. I gave one an earthworm, which she promptly seized with her nippers; she then took up a good sized pebble in the nippers of her front pair of walking legs, glided over to the other nest, spitefully threw down both worm and pebble on top of her fellow prisoner, and then sped homeward. Her victim responded to the act by rising up and expressing perfectly, in his attitude and the gestures of his great claws, the most eloquent of crayfish profanity. In watching crayfishes carry pebbles, I have been astonished to see how constantly the larger pair of jaw-feet are used to help pick up and carry the loads.

LESSON

LEADING THOUGHT— The crayfish, or crawfish, as it is sometimes called, has one pair of legs developed into great pincers for seizing and tearing its food and for defending itself from enemies. It can live in mud or water. It belongs to the same animal group as do the insects, and it is a near cousin of the lobster.

METHOD— Place a crayfish in an aquarium (a battery jar or a two-quart Mason jar) in the schoolroom, keeping it in clear water until the pupils have studied its form. It will rise to explore the sides of the aquarium at first, and thus show its mouth parts, legs and swimmerets. Afterwards, place gravel and stone in the bottom of the aquarium, so that it can hide itself in a little cavity which it will make by carrying pebbles from one side. Wash the gravel well before it is put in, so that the water will be unclouded and the children can watch the process of excavation.

Observations—

1. What is there peculiar about the crayfish which makes it difficult to pick it up? Examine one of these great front legs carefully and see how wonderfully it is made. How many parts are there to it? Note how each succeeding part is larger from the body to the claws. Note the tips which form the nippers or chelae, as they are called. How are they armed? How are the gripping edges formed to take hold of an object? How wide can the nippers be opened, and how is this done? Note the two segments behind the great claw and describe how they help the work of the nippers.

2. Study the pair of legs behind the great claws or chelae, and compare the two pairs, segment by segment. How do they differ except as to size? How do the nippers at the end compare with the big ones? Look at the next pair of legs behind these; are they similar? How do the two pairs of hind legs differ in shape from the two pairs in front of them?

3. Look between the great front claws and see if you can find another pair of small legs. Can you see anything more behind or above these little legs?

4. When the crayfish lifts itself up against the side of the jar, study its mouth. Can you see a pair of notched jaws that work sidewise? Can you see two or three pairs of threadlike organs that wave back and forth in and out the mouth?

5. How many legs, in all, has the crayfish? What are the short legs near the mouth used for? What are the great nippers used for? How many legs does the crayfish use when walking? In what order are they moved? Is the hind pair used for pushing? What use does it make of the pincers on the first and second pairs of walking legs?

6. Look at the crayfish from above; the head and the covering of the thorax are soldered together into one piece. When this occurs, the

whole is called a cephalothorax; and the cover is called by the same name as the upper shell of the turtle, the carapace. Can you see where the head is joined to the thorax?

7. Look carefully at the eyes. Describe how they are set. Can they be pushed out or pulled in? Can they be moved in all directions? Of what advantage is this to the crayfish?

8. How many antennae has the crayfish? Describe the long ones and tell how they are used. Do the two short ones on each side come from the same basal segment? These little ones are called the antennules. Describe the antennules of each side and tell how they differ. Can you see the little fingerlike organs which clasp above the antenna and below the antennules on each side of the head? Can these be moved?

9. Look at the crayfish from above. How many segments are there in the abdomen? Note how graceful the shape of each segment. Note that each has a fan-shaped piece down the side. Describe how the edges of the segments along the sides are margined.

10. Of how many pieces is the tail made? Make a sketch of it. How are the pieces bordered? Can the pieces shut and spread out sidewise? Is the tail hinged so it can be lifted up against the back or curled under the body?

11. Look underneath the abdomen and describe the little fringed organs called the swimmerets. How many are there?

12. How does the crayfish swim? With what does it make the stroke? Describe carefully this action of the tail. When it is swimming, does it use its swimmerets? Why do not the many legs and big nippers obstruct the progress of the crayfish, when it is swimming?

13. When does the crayfish use its swimmerets? Do they work so as to push the body backward or forward? Do you know to what use the mother crayfish puts her swimmerets?

14. Do you know how crayfishes breathe? Do you know what they eat and where they find it?

15. Where do you find crayfishes? Where do they like to hide? Do they go headfirst into their hiding place, or do they back in? Do they stand ready to defend their retreat? When you look down into the brook, are the crayfishes usually seen until they move? Why is this?

Where do the crayfishes pass the winter? Did you ever see the crayfish burrows or mud chimnies?

16. If the crayfish loses one of its legs or antennas, does it grow out again? How does the crayfish grow?

17. Put a crayfish in an aquarium which has three inches of coarse gravel on the bottom, and watch it make its den. How does it loosen up a stone? With how many legs does it carry its burden of pebbles when digging its cave? How does it use its jaw-feet, its nippers, and its first and second pairs of walking legs in this work?

> "A rock-lined, wood-embosomed nook,
> Dim cloister of the chanting brook!
> A chamber within the channelled hills,
> Where the cold crystal brims and spills,
> By dark-browed caverns blackly flows.
> Falls from the cleft like crumbling snows,
> And purls and splashes, breathing round
> A soft, suffusing mist of sound."
>
> —J. T. TROWBRIDGE.

Daddy longlegs

Daddy-Longlegs, or Grandfather Greybeard

TEACHER'S STORY

WONDER if there ever was a country child who has not grasped firmly the leg of one of these little sprawling creatures and demanded: "Grandfather Greybeard, tell me where the cows are or I'll kill you," and Grandfather Greybeard, striving to get away, puts out one of his long legs this way, and another that way, and points in so many directions that he usually saves his life, since the cows must be somewhere. It would be more interesting to the children and less embarrassing to the "daddy" if they were taught to look more closely at those slender, hairlike legs.

"Daddy's" long legs are seven jointed. The first segment is seemingly soldered fast to the lower side of his body, and is called the coxa. The next segment is a mere knob, usually black and ornamental, and is called the trochanter. Then comes the femur, a rather long segment directed upward; next is a short swollen segment—the "knee joint" or patella; next the tibia, which is also rather long. Then comes the metatarsus and tarsus, which seemingly make one long downward-directed segment, outcurving at the tips, on which the "daddy" tip-toes along.

174

I have seen a "daddy" walk into a drop of water and his foot was never wetted, so light was his touch on the water surface film. The second pair of legs is the longest; the fourth pair next, and the first pair usually the shortest. The legs of the second pair are ordinarily used in exploring the surroundings. Notice that, when the "daddy" is running, these two legs are spread wide apart and keep in rapid motion; their tips, far more sensitive than any nerves of our own, tell him the nature of his surroundings, by a touch so light that we cannot feel it on the hand. We have more respect for one of these hairlike legs, when we know it is capable of transmitting intelligence from its tip.

The "daddy" is a good traveler and moves with remarkable rapidity. And why not? If our legs were as long in comparison as his, they would be about forty feet in length. When the "daddy" is running, the body is always held a little distance above the ground; but when the second pair of legs suggests to him that there may be something good to eat in the neighborhood, he commences a peculiar teetering motion of the body, apparently touching it to the ground at every step; as the body is carried tilted with the head down, this movement enables the creature to explore the surface below him with his palpi, which he ordinarily carries bent beneath his face, with the ends curled up under his "chin." The palpi have four segments that are easily seen, and although they are ordinarily carried bent up beneath the head, they can be extended out quite a distance if "daddy" wishes to test a substance. The end segment of the palpus is tipped with a single claw

Beneath the palpi is a pair of jaws; these, in some species, extend beyond the palpi. I have seen a daddy-longlegs hold food to his jaws with his palpi and he seemed also to use them for stuffing it into his mouth.

The body of the

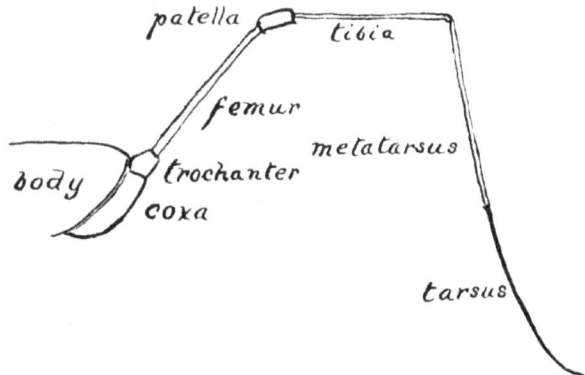

One of "daddy's" long legs with segments named

daddy-longlegs is a little oblong object, looking more like a big grain of wheat than anything else, because in these creatures the head, thorax and abdomen are all grown together compactly. On top of the body, between the feeler-legs, is a little black dot, and to the naked eye it would seem that if this were an organ of sight the creature must be a Cyclops with only one eye. But under the lens this is seen to be a raised knob and there is on each side of it, a little shining black eye. We hardly see the use of two eyes set so closely together, but probably the "daddy" does.

The most entertaining thing which a "daddy" in captivity is likely to do, is to clean his legs; he is very particular about his legs, and he will grasp one close to the basal joint in his jaws and slowly pull it through, meanwhile holding the leg up to the jaws with the palpi, while he industriously nibbles it clean for the whole length to the very toe. Owing to the likelihood of his losing one of his legs, he has the power of growing a new one; so we often see a "daddy" with one or more legs only half grown.

There are many species of daddy-longlegs in the United States, and some of them do not have the characteristic long legs. In the North, all except one species die at the approach of winter; but not until after the female, which, by the way, ought to be called "granny-longlegs," has laid her eggs in the ground, or under some protecting stone, or in some safe crevice of wood or bark. In the spring the eggs hatch into tiny little creatures which look just like the old daddy-longlegs, except for their size. They get their growth like insects, by shedding their skins as fast as they outgrow them. It is interesting to study one of these cast skins with a lens. There it stands with a slit down its back, and with the skin of each leg absolutely perfect to the tiny claw! Again we marvel at these legs that seem so threadlike, and which have an outer covering that can be shed. Some say that the daddy-longlegs live on small insects which they straddle over and pounce down upon, and some say they feed upon decaying matter and vegetable juices. This would be an interesting line of investigation for pupils, since they might be able to give many new facts about the food of these creatures. The "daddies" are night prowlers, and like to hide in crevices by day, waiting for the dark to hunt for their food. They have several common names. Besides the two given they are called "harvestmen" and the French call them "haymakers." Both of these names were very probably given, because the creatures appear in greater numbers at the time of haying and harvesting.

LESSON

LEADING THOUGHT— These long-legged creatures have one pair of legs too many to allow them to be classed with the insects. They are more nearly related to the spiders, who also have eight legs. They are pretty creatures when examined closely, and they do many interesting things.

METHOD— Put a grandfather greybeard in a breeding cage or under a large tumbler, and let the pupils observe him at leisure. If you place a few drops of sweetened water at one side of the cage, the children will surely have an opportunity to see this amusing creature clean his legs.

OBSERVATIONS—

1. Where did you find the harvestman? What did it do as soon as it was disturbed? How many names do you know for this little creature?

2. A "daddy" with such long legs certainly ought to have them studied. How many segments in each leg? How do the segments look? How do the legs look where they are fastened to the body? Which is the longest pair of legs? The next? The next? The shortest?

3. If you had such long stilts as he has, they would be about forty feet long. Would you lift yourself that high in the air? Does the "daddy" lift his body high or swing it near the ground? What shape is the body? Can you see if there is a distinct head? Can you see a black dot on top of the front end of the body? If you should see this dot through a microscope it would prove to be two bright black eyes. Why should the daddy's eyes be on top?

4. Do you see a pair of organs that look like feelers at the front end of the body? These are called palpi. How does he use his palpi? Give him a little bruised or decaying fruit, and see him eat. Where do you think his mouth is? Where does he keep his palpi when he is not using them for eating?

5. Note what care he takes of his legs. How does he clean them? Which does he clean the oftenest? Do you think the very long second pair of legs is used as much for feeling as for walking? Put some object in front of the "daddy" and see him explore it with his legs. How much of the leg is used as a foot when the "daddy" stands or runs?

6. When running fast, how does the "daddy" carry his body? When exploring how does he carry it? Do you ever find the "daddy" with his body resting on the surface on which he is standing? When resting, are all eight of his legs on the ground? Which are in the air? Is the head end usually tilted up or down?

7. Do you see the daddy-longlegs early in the spring? When do you find him most often? How do you suppose he passes the winter in our climate? Have you ever seen a "daddy" with one leg much shorter than the other? How could you explain this?

8. Try and discover what the daddy-longlegs eats, and where he finds his food.

The poisonous black widow or hourglass spider. It and the tarantula are the only dangerous spiders in the United States. Notice the red hourglass on its belly

Spiders

TEACHER'S STORY

THE spiders are the civil engineers among the small inhabitants of our fields and woods. They build strong suspension bridges, from which they hang nets made with exquisite precision; and they build aeroplanes and balloons, which are more efficient than any that we have yet constructed; for although they are not exactly dirigible, yet they carry the little balloonists where they wish to go, and there are few fatal accidents. Moreover, the spiders are of much economic importance, since they destroy countless millions of insects every year, most of which are noxious—like flies, mosquitoes, bugs and grasshoppers.

There is an impression abroad that all spiders are dangerous to handle. This is a mistake; the bite of any of our common spiders is not nearly so dangerous as the bite of a malaria-laden mosquito. Although there is a little venom injected into the wound by the bite of any spider, yet there is no species found in the Northern States whose bite is sufficiently venomous to be feared.

There is no need for studying the anatomy of the spider closely in nature-study. Our interest lies much more in the wonderful structures made by the spiders,

The tarantula, a large, dark-colored, hairy spider found in the Southwest. It is poisonous

than in a detailed study of the little creatures themselves.

Cobwebs
"Here shy Arachne winds her endless thread.
And weaves her silken tapestry unseen,
Veiling the rough-hewn timbers overhead.
And looping gossamer festoons between."
—ELIZABETH AKERS.

Our house spiders are indefatigable curtain-weavers. We never suspect their presence, until suddenly their curtains appear before our eyes, in the angles of the ceilings—invisible until laden with dust. The cobwebs are made of crisscrossed lines, which are so placed as to entangle any fly that comes near. The lines are stayed to the sides of the wall and to each other quite firmly, and thus they are able to hold a fly that touches them. The spider is likely to be in its little den at the side of the web; this den may be in a crevice in the corner or in a tunnel made of the silk. As soon as a fly becomes entangled in the web the spider runs to it, seizes it in its jaws, sucks its blood, and then throws away the shell, the wings and legs. If a spider is frightened, it at first tries to hide and then may drop by a thread to the floor. If we catch the little acrobat it will usually "play possum" and we may examine it more closely through a lens. We shall find it is quite different in form

A black and yellow garden spider.

from an insect. First to be noted, it has eight legs; but most important of all, it has only two parts to the body. The head and thorax are consolidated into one piece, which is called the cephalothorax. The abdomen has no segments like that of the insects, and is joined to the cephalothorax by a short, narrow stalk. At the front of the head is the mouth, guarded by two mandibles, each ending in a sharp claw, at the tip of which the poison gland opens. It is by thrusting these mandibles into its prey that it kills its victims. On each side of the mandible is a palpus, which in the males is of very strange shape. The eyes are situated on the top of the head. There are usually four pairs of these eyes, and each looks as beady and alert as if it were the only one.

The spinning organs of the spider are situated near the tip of the abdomen, while the spinning organ of the caterpillar is situated near its lower lip. The spider's silk comes from two or three pairs of spinnerets which are fingerlike in form, and upon the end of each are many small tubes from which the silk is spun. The silk is in a fluid state as it issues from the spinnerets, but it hardens immediately on contact with the air. In making their webs, spiders produce two kinds of silk, one is dry and

A banana spider.

inelastic, making the framework of the web; the other is sticky and elastic, clinging to anything that it touches. The body and the legs of spiders are usually hairy.

LESSON

LEADING THOUGHT— The cobwebs which are found in the corners of ceilings and in other dark places in our houses, are made by the house spider which spins its web in these situations for the purpose of catching insects.

A female jumping spider.

METHOD—The pupils should have under observation a cobweb in a corner of a room, preferably with a spider in it.

OBSERVATIONS—

1. Is the web in a sheet or is it a mass of crisscrossed, tangled threads? How are the threads held in place?

2. What is the purpose of this web? Where does the spider hide? Describe its den.

3. If a fly becomes tangled in a web, describe the action of the spider. Does the spider eat all of the fly? What does it do with the remains?

4. If the spider is frightened, what does it do? Where does the silken thread come from, and how does its source differ from the source of the silken thread spun by caterpillars?

5. Imprison a spider under a tumbler or in a vial, and look at it very carefully. How many legs has it? How does the spider differ from insects in this respect? How many sections are there to the body? How does the spider differ from insects in this respect?

6. Look closely at the head. Can you see the hooked jaws, or fangs? Can you see the palpi on each side of the jaws? Where are the spider's eyes? How many pairs has it?

When the tangled cobweb pulls
The cornflower's cap awry.
And the lilies tall lean over the wall
To bow to the butterfly
It is July.

—SUSAN HARTLEY SWETT.

The spiny-bellied spider

The funnel web of a grass spider

The Funnel Web

"And dew-bright webs festoon the grass
In roadside fields at morning."
—ELIZABETH AKERS.

SOMETIMES on a dewy morning, a field will seem carpeted with these webs, each with its opening stretched wide, and each with its narrow hallway of retreat. The general shape of the web is like that of a broad funnel with a tube leading down at one side. This tube is used as a hiding place for the spider, which thus escapes the eyes of its enemies, and also keeps out of sight of any insects that might be frightened at seeing it, and so avoid the web. But the tube is no cul-de-sac; quite to the contrary, it has a rear exit, through which the spider, if frightened, escapes from attack.

The web is formed of many lines of silk crossing each other irregularly, forming a firm sheet. This sheet is held in place by many guy-lines, which fasten it to surrounding objects. If the web is touched lightly, the spider rushes forth from its lair to seize its prey; but if the web be jarred roughly, the spider speeds out through its back door and can be found only with difficulty. The smaller insects of the field, such as flies and bugs, are the chief food of this spider; it rarely attempts to seize a grown grasshopper.

The funnel-shaped webs in dark corners of cellars are made by a species which is closely related to the grass spider and has the same general habits, but which builds in these locations instead of in the grass.

LESSON

LEADING THOUGHT—The grass spider spins funnel-shaped webs in the grass to entrap the insects of the field. This web has a back door.

METHOD—Ask the pupils to observe a web on the grass with a spider within it.

OBSERVATIONS—

1. What is the general shape of the web? Is there a tunnel leading down from it? Why is it called a funnel web?

2. Of what use is the funnel tube, and what is its shape? Where does it lead, and of what use is it to the spider? Can you corner a spider in its funnel tube? Why not?

3. How is the web made? Is there any regularity in the position of the threads that make it? How is it stayed in place?

4. Touch the web lightly, and note how the spider acts. Jar the web roughly, and what does the spider do?

5. What insects become entangled in this web?

6. Compare this web with similar funnel webs found in corners of cellars, sheds or piazzas, and see if you think the same kind of spider made both.

An orb web on a dewy morning

The Orb-Web

OF all the structures made by the lower creatures, the orb-web of the spider is, beyond question, the most intricate and beautiful in design, and the most exquisite in workmanship. The watching of the construction of one of these webs is an experience that brings us close to those mysteries which seem to be as fundamental as they are inexplicable in the plan of the universe. It is akin to watching the growth of a crystal, or the stars wheeling across the heavens in their appointed courses.

The orb-web of the large, black and yellow garden spider is, perhaps, the best subject for this study, although many of the smaller orbs are far more delicate in structure. These orb-webs are most often placed vertically, since they are thus more likely to be in the path of flying insects. The number of radii, or spokes, differs with the different species of spiders, and they are usually fastened to a silken framework, which in turn is fastened by guy-lines to surrounding objects. These radii or spokes are connected by a continuous spiral line, spaced regularly except at the center or hub; this hub or center is of more solid silk, and is usually surrounded by an open space; and it may be merely an irregular network, or it may have wide bands of silk laid across it.

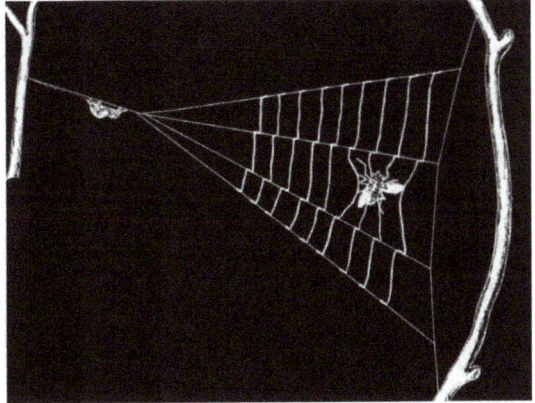

The finished web of a triangle spider

The radii or spokes, the guy-lines, the framework and the center of the web are all made of inelastic silk, which does not adhere to an object that touches it. The spiral line, on the contrary, is very elastic, and adheres to any object brought in contact with it. An insect which touches one of these spirals and tries to escape, becomes entangled in the neighboring lines and is thus held fast until the spider can reach it. If one of these elastic lines be examined with a microscope, it is a most beautiful object. There are strung upon it, like pearls, little drops of sticky fluid, which render it not only elastic but adhesive.

Some species of orbweavers remain at the center of the web, while others hide in some little retreat near at hand. If in the middle, the spider always keeps watchful claws upon the radii of the web so that if there is any jarring of the structure by an entrapped insect, it is at once apprised of the fact; if the

The triangle spider usually rests on the single line of the web

spider is in a den at one side, it keeps a claw upon a trap line which is stretched tightly from the hub of the web to the den, and thus communicates any vibration of the web to the hidden sentinel. When the insect becomes entangled, the spider rushes out and envelops it in a band of silk, which feat it accomplishes, by turning the insect over and over rapidly, meanwhile spinning a broad, silken band which swathes it. It may bite the insect before it begins to swathe it in silk, or afterwards. It usually hangs the swathed insect to the

Some of the orb weavers strengthen their orb webs by spinning a zigzag ribbon, as pictured above, across the center

web near where it was caught, until ready to eat it; it then takes the prey to the center of the web, if there is where the spider usually sits, or to its den at one side, if it is a den-making species, and there sucks the insect's blood, carefully throwing away the hard parts.

The spider does not become entangled in the web, because, when it runs it steps upon the dry radii and not upon the sticky spiral lines. During the busy season, the spider is likely to make a new web every twenty-four hours, but this depends largely upon whether the web has meanwhile been destroyed by large insects.

The spider's method of making its first bridge is to place itself upon some high point and, lifting its abdomen in the air, to spin out on the

The spinner of this web, Abaurobius, lives in a crevice in the cliff. The web was spun about the entrance.

breeze a thread of silk. When this touches any object, it adheres, and the spider draws in the slack until the line is "taut;" it then travels across this bridge, which is to support its web, and makes it stronger by doubling the line. From this line, it stretches other lines by fastening a thread to one point, and then walking along to some other point, spinning the thread as it goes and holding the line clear of the object on which it is walking by means of one of its hind legs. When the right point is reached, it pulls the line tight, fastens it, and then, in a similar fashion,

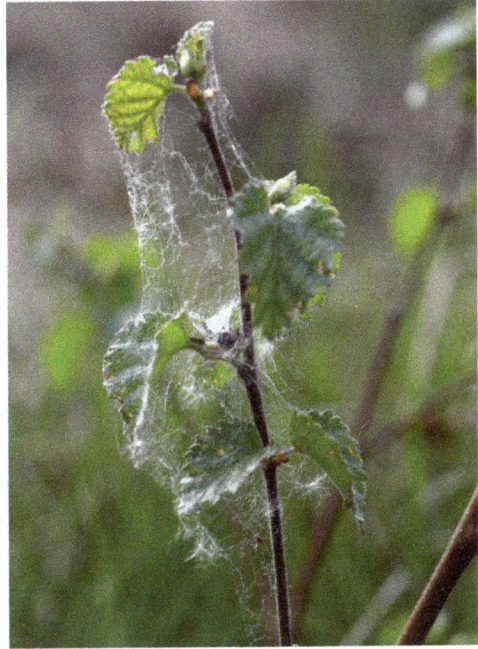

The irregular web of a dictynid

proceeds to make another. It may make its first radius by dropping from its bridge to some point below; then climbing back to the center, it fastens the line for another radius, and spinning as it goes, walks down and out to some other point, holding the thread clear and then pulling it tight before fastening it. Having thus selected the center of the web, it goes back and forth to and from it, spinning lines until all of the radii are completed and fastened at one center. It then starts at the center and spins a spiral, laying it onto the radii to hold them firm. However, the lines of this spiral are farther apart and much more irregular than the final spiral. Thus far, all of the threads the spider has spun are inelastic and not sticky; and this first, or temporary spiral is used by the spider to walk upon when spinning the final spiral. It begins the latter at the outer edge instead of at the center, and works toward the middle. As the second spiral progresses, the spider with its jaws cuts away the spiral which it first made, and which it has used as a scaffolding. A careful observer may often see remnants of this first spiral on the radii between the lines of the permanent spiral. The spider works very rapidly and will complete a web in a very short time. The final spiral is made of the elastic and adhesive silk.

References— Comstock's Manual; Common Spiders, Emerton; The Spider Book, Comstock; Nature's Craftsmen, McCook.

LESSON

LEADING THOUGHT— No structure made by a creature lower than man is so exquisitely perfect as the orb-web of the spider.

METHOD— There should be an orb-web where the pupils can observe it, preferably with the spider in attendance.

OBSERVATIONS—

1. Is the orb-web usually hung horizontally or vertically?

2. Observe the radii, or "spokes," of the web. How many are there? How are they fastened to surrounding objects? Is each spoke fastened to some object or to a framework of silken lines?

3. Observe the silken thread laid around the spokes. Is it a spiral line or is each circle complete? Are the lines the same distance apart on the outer part of the web as at the center? How many of the circling lines are there?

4. Is the center of the web merely an irregular net, or are there bands of silk put on in zigzag shape?

5. Touch any of the "spokes" lightly with the point of a pencil. Does it adhere to the pencil and stretch out as you pull the pencil away? Touch one of the circling lines with a pencil point, and see if it adheres to the point and is elastic. What is the reason for this difference in the stickiness and elasticity of the different kinds of silk in the orb-web?

6. If an insect touches the web, how does it become more entangled by seeking to get away?

7. Where does the spider stay, at the center of the web or in a little retreat at one side?

8. If an insect becomes entangled in the web, how does the spider discover the fact and act?

9. If the spider sits at the middle of the orb, it has a different method for discovering when an insert strikes the web than does the spider that hides in a den at one side. Describe the methods of each.

10. How does the spider make fast an insect? Does it bite the insect before it envelops it in silk? Where does it carry the insect to feed upon it?

11. How does the spider manage to run about its web without becoming entangled in the sticky thread? How often does the orb-weaver make a new web?

How an Orb-Web Is Made

Spiders may be seen making their webs in the early morning or in the evening. Find an orb-web with a spider in attendance; break the web without frightening the spider and see it replace it in the early evening, or in the morning about daybreak. An orb-weaver may be brought into the house on its web, when the web is on a branch, and placed where it will not be disturbed, and thus be watched at leisure.

OBSERVATIONS—

1. How does the spider manage to place the supporting line between two points?

2. How does it make the framework for holding the web in place?

3. How does it make the first radius?

4. How does it make the other radii and select the point which is to be the center of the web?

5. How does it keep the line which it is spinning clear of the line it walks upon?

A partially completed orb-web.
a. the temporary spiral stay line; b. the sticky spiral line; c. the fragments of the temporary spiral hanging in a radius.

6. After the radii are all made, are they fastened at the center?

7. How and where does the spider first begin to spin a spiral? Are the lines of this spiral close together or far apart? For what is the first spiral used?

8. Where does it begin to spin the permanent spiral? Where does it walk when spinning it? By the way it walks on the first spiral, do you

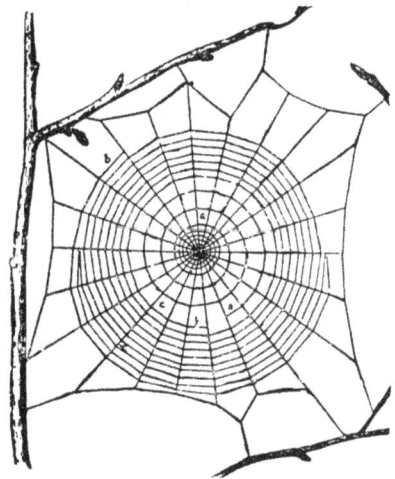

think it is sticky and elastic? What does it do with the first spiral while the second one is being finished?

9. If the center of the web has a zigzag ribbon of silk, when was it put on?

10. How many minutes did it take the spider to complete the web?

Supplementary reading— "Argiope of the Silver Shield," Insect Stories, Kellogg.

A filmy dome web with its maker

The Filmy Dome

TEACHER'S STORY

LIKE bubbles cut in half, these delicate domes catch the light rays and separate them like a prism into waves of rainbow colors. One of these domes is usually about the size of an ordinary bowl, and is suspended with the opening on the lower side. It is held in place by many guy-lines which attach it to surrounding objects. Above a filmy dome are always stretched many crisscrossed threads for some distance up. These are for the purpose of hindering the flight of insects, so that they will fall into the web. The little spider, which always hangs, back downward, just below the center of the dome, rushes to its prey from the lower side, pulls it through the meshes of the web, and feeds upon it. But any remains of the insect or pieces of sticks or leaves which may drop upon the web, it carefully cuts out and drops to the ground, mending the hole very neatly.

LESSON

LEADING THOUGHT— One little spider spins a filmy dome, beneath the apex of which it hangs, back downward, awaiting its prey.

METHOD— On a sunny day in late summer or early autumn, while walking along woodland paths, the careful observer is sure to see suspended among the bushes or in the tops of weeds, or among dead branches of young hemlocks, the filmy dome webs. They are about as large as a small bowl, and usually so delicate that they cannot be seen unless the sun shines upon them; they are likely to be exquisitely iridescent under the sun's rays. Such a dome may be studied by a class or by the pupils individually.

OBSERVATIONS—

1. Where did you discover the filmy dome? What is the size of the dome? Does it open above or below? How is it held in place?

2. Are there many crisscrossed threads extending above the dome? If so, what do you think they are for?

3. Where does the spider stay? Is the spider large and heavy, or small and delicate?

4. What does the spider do if an insect becomes entangled in its web?

5. Throw a bit of stick or leaf upon a filmy dome web, and note what becomes of it.

> *"With spiders I had friendship made.*
> *And watch'd them in their sullen trade."*
> —*PRISONER OF CHILLON.*

A sea of gossamer. The webs of ballooning spiders

Ballooning Spiders

TEACHER'S STORY

IF we look across the grass some warm sunny morning or evening of early fall, we see threads of spider silk clinging everywhere; these are not regular webs for trapping insects, but are single threads spun from grass stalk to grass stalk until the fields are carpeted with glistening silk. We have a photograph of a plowed field, taken in autumn, which looks likes the waves of a lake; so completely is the ground covered with spider threads that it shows the "path of the sun" like water.

When we see so many of these random threads, it is a sign that the young spiders have started on their travels, and it is not difficult then to find one in the act. The spiderling climbs up some tall object, like a twig or a blade of grass, and sends out its thread of silk upon the air. If the thread becomes entangled, the spiderling sometimes walks off on it, using it as a bridge, or sometimes it begins again. If the thread does not become entangled with any object, there is soon enough given off, so that the friction of the air current upon it supports the weight of the body of the little creature, which promptly lets go its hold of earth as soon as it feels safely buoyed up, and off it floats to lands unknown. Spiders thus sailing through the air have been discovered in mid-ocean.

Thus we see that the spiders have the same way of distributing their species over the globe, as have the thistles and dandelions. It has been asked what the spiders live upon while they are making these long journeys, especially those that have drifted out to sea. The spider has very convenient habits of eating. When it finds plenty of food it eats a great deal; but in time of famine it lives on, apparently comfortably, without eating. One of our captive spiders was mislaid for six months and when we found her she was as full of "grit" as ever, and she did not seem to be abnormally hungry when food was offered her.

> "A noiseless, patient spider,
> I mark'd where, on a little promontory, it stood isolated:
> Mark'd how to explore the vacant, vast surrounding.
> It launched forth filament out of itself
> Ever unreeling them—ever tirelessly speeding them.
> "And you, my soul, where you stand,
> Surrounded, surrounded, in measureless oceans of space.
> Ceaselessly, musing, venturing, throwing,
> seeking the spheres to connect them;
> Till the bridge you will need be form'd—
> till the ductile anchor hold;
> Till the gossamer thread you fling catch somewhere,
> O my soul."
>
> —WALT WHITMAN.

LESSON

LEADING THOUGHT— The young of many species of spiders scatter themselves like thistle seeds in balloons which they make of silk.

METHOD—These observations should be made out of doors during some warm sunny day in October. Read Nature's Craftsmen, McCook, p. 182.

OBSERVATIONS—

1. Look across the grass some warm sunny morning or evening of early fall, and note the threads of spider silk gleaming everywhere,

not regular webs, but single threads spun from grass stalk to grass stalk, or from one object to another, until the ground seems glistening with silk threads.

2. Find a small spider on a bush, fence post, or at the top of some tall grass stalk; watch it until it begins to spin out its thread.

3. What happens to the thread as it is spun out?

4. If the thread does not become entangled in any surrounding object what happens? If the thread does become entangled, what happens?

5. How far do you suppose a spider can travel on this silken aeroplane? Why should the young spider wish to travel?

The white crab spider

The White Crab-Spider

TEACHER'S STORY

THERE are certain spiders which are crablike in form, and their legs are so arranged that they can walk more easily sidewise or backward than forward. These spiders spin no webs, but lie in wait for their prey. Many of them live upon plants and fences and, in winter, hide in protected places.

The white crab-spider is a little rascal that has discovered the advantage of protective coloring as a means of hiding itself from the view of its victims, until too late to save themselves; the small assassin always takes on the color of the flower in which it lies concealed. In the white trillium, it is greenish white; while in the golden-rod its decorations are yellow. It waits in the heart of the flower, or in the flower clusters, until the visiting insect alights and seeks to probe for the nectar; it then leaps forward and fastens its fangs into its struggling victim. I have seen a crab-spider in a milkweed attack a bee three times its size. This spider was white with lilac or purple markings. If disturbed, the crab-spider can walk off awkwardly or it may drop by a silken thread. It is especially interesting, since it illustrates another use for protective coloring; and also because this species seems to be able to change its colors to suit its surroundings.

LESSON

LEADING THOUGHT— The white crab spider has markings upon its body of the same color as the flower in which it rests and is thus enabled to hide in ambush out of the sight of

CHINMAYISK (CC BY-SA 3.0)
A white crab spider preying on a butterfly

its victims—the insects which come to the flower for nectar.

METHOD— Ask the children to bring one of these spiders to school in the flower in which it was found; note how inconspicuous it is, and arouse an interest in the different colors which these spiders assume in different flowers.

OBSERVATIONS—

1. What is the shape of the body of the crab-spider? Which of the legs are the longest? Are these legs directed forward or backward?

2. How is the body marked? What colors do you find upon it? Are the colors the same in the spiders found in the trilliums, as those in other flowers? Why is this? Do you think that the color of the spider keeps it from being seen?

3. Place the white spider which you may find in a trillium in a daffodil, and note if the color changes.

4. Do the crab-spiders make webs? How do they trap their prey?

199

How the Spider Mothers
Take Care of Their Eggs

TEACHER'S STORY

PROTECTING her eggs from the vicissitudes of the weather seems to be the spider mother's chief care; though at the same time and by the same means, she protects them from the attacks of predacious insects. Many of the species make silken egg-sacs, which are often elaborate in construction, and are carefully placed in protected situations.

Often a little silvery disk may be seen attached to a stone in a field. It resembles a circular lichen on the stone, but if it is examined it is found to consist of an upper, very smooth, waterproof coat, while below is a soft, downy nest, completely enfolding the spider's eggs.

INGRID TAYLAR (CC BY-SA 2.0)
Entrance to the underground nest of a turret spider

The egg-sacs of the cobweb weavers are often found suspended in their webs. One of the large orb-weavers makes a very remarkable nest, which it attaches to the branches of weeds or shrubs. This sac is about as large as a hickory nut, and opens like a vase at the top. It is very securely suspended by many strong threads of silk, so that the blasts of winter cannot tear it loose. The outside is shining and waterproof, while inside it has a fit lining for a spiderling cradle.

Dr. Burt G. Wilder studied the development of the inmates of one of these nests by cutting open different nests at different periods of the winter. In the autumn, the nest contained five hundred or more eggs. These eggs hatched in early winter but it seemed foreordained that some of the little spiders were born for food for their stronger brethren. They seemed resigned to their fate, for when one of these victims was seized by its cannibalistic brother, it curled up its legs and submitted meekly. The result of this process was that, out of the five hundred little spiders hatched from the eggs, only a few healthy and apparently happy young spiders emerged from the nest in the spring, sustained by the nourishment afforded them by their own family, and fitted for their life in the outside world.

Some spiders make a nest for their eggs within folded leaves, and some build them in crevices of rocks and boards.

The running spiders, which are the large ones found under stones, make globular egg-sacs; the mother spider drags after her this egg-sac attached to her spinnerets; the young, when they hatch, climb upon their mother's back, and there remain for a time.

IAN W. FIEGGEN (CC BY-SA 2.0)
Wolf spider carrying egg sac

WOCKY (CC BY-SA 3.0)
Female Latrodectus hasselti *guarding egg sac*

MARSHAL HEDIN (CC BY-SA 2.0)
The trap-door spider nest. The spider digs a tunnel in the ground, coats the walls with earth and saliva, and then spins a lining of silk. The hinged door is a continuation of the walls with the outer surface covered with earth

201

A california trapdoor spider

This female Priestly Spiny Orb-weaver (Gasteracantha sacerdotalis) *built its egg-sac on a shiny glass surface*

LESSON

LEADING THOUGHT— The spider mothers have many interesting ways of protecting their eggs, which they envelop in silken sacs and place in safety.

METHOD— Ask the pupils to bring in all the spider egg-sacs that they can find. Keep some of them unopened, and open others of the same kind, and thus discover how many eggs are in the sac, and how many spiderlings come out. This is a good lesson for September and October.

OBSERVATIONS—

1. In what situation did you find the nest? How was it protected from rain and snow? To what was it attached?

2. Of what texture is the outside of the sac? Is the outside made of waterproof silk? What is the texture of the lining?

202

3. How many eggs in this sac? What is the color of the eggs? When do the spiderlings hatch? Do as many spiders come out of the sac as there were eggs? Why is this?